The Man You Can Be For The 21st Century

The Man You Can Be For The 21st Century

This book presents a new vision of masculinity.

J.D. Lee

Illustrated by Keith Klein

© 2017 J.D. Lee
All rights reserved.

ISBN: 1547107413
ISBN 13: 9781547107414

TABLE OF CONTENTS

FOR MEN—AND ONLY FOR MEN · · · · · · · · · · · · · · · · 1
   Men Make Men · 2
   Young Men Want Answers · · · · · · · · · · · · · · · · 3
   Man's Language Used Here · · · · · · · · · · · · · · · 4

THE KICKER · 6
   Advice Is Not Enough · · · · · · · · · · · · · · · · · · 7
   Do What Works for You · · · · · · · · · · · · · · · · · · 9
   Benefits of Higher Standards · · · · · · · · · · · · · 9
   What Serves You and What Screws You · · · · · · · · · · ·11

**THE CORE OF MANHOOD: FATHER,
SEXUALITY, AND WORK** ·13
   The Male's Silent Hunger for the Father · · · · · · · · ·13
   Delinquent Elephants · · · · · · · · · · · · · · · · · · ·14
   What Happens to the Male's Psyche When
   the Father Is Not Around? · · · · · · · · · · · · · · · · ·16

THE WAY TO MANHOOD · · · · · · · · · · · · · · · · · · ·19
    Step One: Fathering Yourself· · · · · · · · · · · · · · · · · ·19
    Step Two: Fathering Yourself If Your Father Is Around · · ·20
    Step Three: Fathering Yourself If Your Father Is Absent · ·21
    Step Four: Taking Action · · · · · · · · · · · · · · · · · ·23

THE BENEFITS OF A MENTOR · · · · · · · · · · · · · · · ·24
    Finding a Mentor ·25
    The Sexes: The Male and Female Genders· · · · · · · · ·26
    Male, Female: Opposites or Both? · · · · · · · · · · · ·27
    Sex: The Act! (It Gets better as You Get Older) · · · · ·29
    Taking Action ·30
    Overcoming Being Shy · · · · · · · · · · · · · · · · · · ·31
    Improving Understanding· · · · · · · · · · · · · · · · · ·32
    When She Catches Your Eye · · · · · · · · · · · · · · · ·34
    Rejection Is Part of the Game · · · · · · · · · · · · · · ·35

DECODING THE FEMALE: BASICS FOR THE MALE · · ·37
    Her "Yes" and Her "No" · · · · · · · · · · · · · · · · · ·37
    She's Not Lying· ·39
    When a "No" Can Be Dangerous · · · · · · · · · · · · ·41
    The Female: Basics Every Man Should Know · · · · · · ·42
        Fantasy #1 ·42
        Fantasy #2 · 44

THE 21ST CENTURY WOMAN AND YOU:
SEARCHING AND INDEPENDENT · · · · · · · · · · · ·46
    Women Today Have Many Options · · · · · · · · · · · ·47
    Women Today Have a Lot to Offer · · · · · · · · · · · ·47
    The Career Female: You Are Not on Her Shopping List· ·48
    The Dating Dilemma ·49

Boring Men Do Not Please the Modern Female · · · · · ·50
Taking Action: Manners ·52
Being Polite: The Basics · · · · · · · · · · · · · · · · · · ·52
The Female Nucleus of Inner Being: To Be
Loved and Receptive· ·53
The Male Nucleus of Inner Being: To Love, to
Achieve, to Give ·54

THREE REALITIES OF THE 21ST CENTURY IMPACTING MEN TO CHANGE· · · · · · · · · · · · · · · · · ·56
Men's Positions in Modern Society· · · · · · · · · · · · ·56
Measures of Men's Losses of Power · · · · · · · · · · · ·57
Men Commit Suicide Five Times More than Women · ·58
Longevity and Health ·60
Women Are Outperforming Men · · · · · · · · · · · · · ·62
The Patriarchy Is Dead ·63
Another Kick to the Balls: The Media · · · · · · · · · · ·63
Enough with Male Bashing · · · · · · · · · · · · · · · · · ·64
Media Outlets for Men ·65
Overcompensation ·65
Battling the Bashing: The Way of the 21st Century Man · ·66

THE EVOLVING 21ST CENTURY· · · · · · · · · · · · · · · · ·68
Scattered Thinking· ·69
Going Backward· ·69
Shifts in the 21st Century· · · · · · · · · · · · · · · · · · · ·70
Skilled, Motivated, and Low-Wage Billions· · · · · · · ·71
Computers and "Thinking" Robots · · · · · · · · · · · · ·71
The Internet· ·73
Overpopulation and Megacities· · · · · · · · · · · · · · ·73
More Working Years ·74

Capitalism, Abundance, and Meaning · · · · · · · · · · · ·75
The Years 2020 and 2024: More Uncertain Changes · · ·76
21st Century America: The Loss of the American
Dream(er) ·78
Class Society: Few on the Top · · · · · · · · · · · · · · · ·79
Control and the Cost of an Education · · · · · · · · · · · ·80

THE FULL IMPACT: IT IS GETTING HARDER · · · · · ·82
Changes Offer New Opportunities · · · · · · · · · · · · · ·83
Cashing In on the Opportunities · · · · · · · · · · · · · · ·84
Learning to Learn ·84
Measure of the 21st Century Man · · · · · · · · · · · · · · ·86
The Man for the 21st Century: Whole,
Connected, Strong ·87
Old Ideals of Manhood ·88
It Can Be Summed Up by the Three P's:
Provide, Protect, Procreate · · · · · · · · · · · · · · · · · 90

THE THREE STANDARD TYPES OF MALES AND THE 21ST CENTURY, 4TH DIMENSIONAL MAN · · · · ·92
The Glorified Male ·92
The Alternative Male ·93
Men of the Opposition ·94

THE ADVANCED, 21ST CENTURY MAN OF 4 DIMENSIONS ·96
21st Century Glorified Male · · · · · · · · · · · · · · · · · ·96
21st Century Alternative Male · · · · · · · · · · · · · · · ·97
21st Century Man of the Opposition · · · · · · · · · · · · ·97

THE RIGHT STATE OF MIND · · · · · · · · · · · · · · · · · ·99
When To #JustSayNo · · · · · · · · · · · · · · · · · · ·99
The Seducer of Seducers: The Digital Media · · · · · · · 100
The Reality Check · 101
The Question: Do Hours of Media Viewing
Help or Retard? · 102
The Choice: Addiction or Addition? · · · · · · · · · · · 103

PLANNING AHEAD: TIMED EVENTS IN A
MAN'S LIFE· 104
The Rule of 72 · 104
Twenties to Thirties: The Start-Up Period · · · · · · · · 105
The Culture's Problem with Young Men · · · · · · · · · 106
Taking Action—The First Step: The Job· · · · · · · · · · 108
Some Habits to Help · · · · · · · · · · · · · · · · · · · 108

THE SECOND STEP: YOUR VISION · · · · · · · · · · · 110
Rituals to Manhood · 111
Rituals to Use· 112
Without a Clear Path, How Does a Young Man
Become Affirmed as a Man? · · · · · · · · · · · · · · · · 113

PLANNING AHEAD, CONTINUED: TIMED
EVENTS TO THE NINETIETH YEAR · · · · · · · · · · 115
Thirties to Forties: Skills Applied· · · · · · · · · · · · · 115
Forty to Forty-Five: No Man Is Exempt· · · · · · · · · · 116
Fifty-Eight to Seventies: One-Third to Go· · · · · · · · · 117
Eighty-Four-Plus: Very Likely! · · · · · · · · · · · · · · 118

THE 21ST CENTURY MAN TAKING ACTION · · · · · 120
The Business of the Body · · · · · · · · · · · · · · · 120
Muscle to the Rescue? · · · · · · · · · · · · · · · · · 121
Clothes Make and Unmake a Man · · · · · · · · · · · 122
Your IQ on Parade: Both Sides of Your
Brain Working Together · · · · · · · · · · · · · · · · 122
The Job You Have and the Job You Want · · · · · · · 124
Taking Action: Notching up Your IQ · · · · · · · · · · 124
Appropriate for the Event · · · · · · · · · · · · · · · 125
Shoes · 125
Style · 126
Grooming: Absolute Turnoffs · · · · · · · · · · · · · 126

LEARNING HOW TO MULTIPLY MONEY · · · · · · · · 128

COLLEGE AND TUITION · · · · · · · · · · · · · · · · · 130
Some Possibilities · · · · · · · · · · · · · · · · · · · 130

THE HUMANITIES FOR INTELLIGENT LIVING · · · 133

LIFELONG LEARNING · · · · · · · · · · · · · · · · · · 137

CONCLUSION · 139

THE 21ST CENTURY WARRIOR · · · · · · · · · · · · 141

RECOMMENDED READING · · · · · · · · · · · · · · · 145

REFERENCES FOR MANNERS AND STYLE · · · · · · · 147

REFERENCES CONCERNING MEN · · · · · · · · · · · · · 149

ACKNOWLEDGMENTS · · · · · · · · · · · · · · · · · · · 153

ABOUT THE AUTHOR · · · · · · · · · · · · · · · · · · 155

INDEX · 159

FOR MEN—AND ONLY FOR MEN

I wrote this book to be read by men and *only* by men, primarily young men in their twenties and early thirties. Why? This decade marks the critical period when a young man becomes an adult male. The pulling apart of past values and ways during these rapidly changing times drives young men to seek direction and guidance. The problem is that young men are getting direction and guidance far too much from women, as well as institutions and policies that favor the feminine and ignore the masculine.

Men Make Men

Women cannot empower masculinity. This isn't an insult to women. Simply put, men make boys into men. Women do not. A male has to follow his male instincts. Women do not have that quality. A young man cannot follow the direction of a female to become a man. He must separate from his mother and be guided by adult men to grow into full manhood.

In primitive and tribal societies, men seize the boys from their mothers to carry them into the company of men so that they become a man among men. The jumps and hurdles a boy needs to overcome are clear in these conservative social systems. The boy will either succeed or fail, thereby earning the respect of those men who taught him, or he will lose honor within his tribe.

The 21st century has created a new paradigm shift, and the criteria are not clear. The standards for manhood have become confused and distorted, and young men are not getting the support they need to grow and thrive. Yet the natural instinct to grow into manhood impels young men to seek ways to affirm themselves as men. Eventually all young men want to say honestly, "I am a man." And more so: "I am a man apart from what society and women tell me I should be." What he does or owns does not solely define him as a man. The inner experience is just as essential as the outer material. Young men need to embrace the growing awareness of their full potential, which can fulfill their dreams and create inner contentment as they mature.

Whether a man is sitting in a leather chair as the boss, is sitting in the seat of an 18-wheeler, plucking on a computer, holding a welding torch, or being a chef, he can say, "I have sense of pride in myself."

Young Men Want Answers

Scores of young men in their twenties to early thirties (and many women, too) have asked me to write my responses about the choices they are planning to make in life: career, marriage, gender identity, understanding the opposite sex, emotional issues, and social and economic changes. Because so many of these young men lacked guidance growing up, yet have such driving forces to become well-rounded and mature men, they sought out my advice and direction.

Thirty years as an educational and school psychologist in Los Angeles allowed me to engage young men from dozens of nationalities. My work with young men from many ethnic and social backgrounds taught me to connect personally to their realities and immediate concerns. I did not have to give them the politically and academically correct spin. They would sense the bull—— a mile away. Nor did I have an academic position to defend. I taught them what was real and urgent for them without using escape clauses to avoid offending the "thought police." I think that these young adults grabbed onto what I put forth because it resonated at a deep and intuitive level. It meant something to them. What I say may twist some heads around because it draws from a broad range of face-to-face and hands-on experience. And that kind of knowledge almost always upsets those who lack the knowledge that real-life experience brings.

What I write is eclectic and personal. I gave these young men a compass so that they may seek their directions. I certainly hope that you will glean that from this book as well. It is truly my desire to teach them that their success internally is just as important as their external achievements.

Man's Language Used Here

Men have a language all their own. It is direct and straight to the point, often blunt and below the belt. What men have to say to one another cannot be said with even one woman present because it will change the language and the dynamic of the conversation. Similarly, when a man is present, it puts women in different modes because young men have especially acute "crap detectors"; their straight and to-the-point language—without the endless qualifiers, exceptions, and loopholes—is inevitably bound to offend some. They get to the truth of the matter and are not easily fooled by deception. We call them "The Leaders."

This will deflect those who are not connected to themselves, who live too much in their heads, who swallow the "politically correct" talk, who are mentally lazy, and who clearly don't question anything. We call them "The Followers."

The Man You Can Be For The 21st Century confronts many outworn beliefs of thinking, thereby creating emotionally charged thought bites that have been in circulation for several decades. Moreover, without any apology, the position of this book is distinctly biased toward the welfare of men. Also, the higher standards of masculinity outlined here add to the

The Man You Can Be For The 21

potential protests against those who hate change, e
it is positive.

The language proposed here sets higher standards of m
culinity and insightful comprehension that empower men.
And empowered men threaten the various entities that take
advantage of the vulnerabilities of weaker men, laid bare
from the gaps that have halted men's proper development.

Cultivating your full self will help you control your own
life and destiny and become independent of external forces
(media, feminization, economics, politics, and legal situations) that don't support your well-being.

THE KICKER

Most recently, I came upon several books on the subject of mothers raising their sons to be men. It was like a slap in the face when I read them. While I certainly understand that there are many women out there raising their sons on their own, I found it somewhat crazy to think that women can teach boys to be men. I knew something had to be done. It made me aware that giving young men guidance to serve their own interests is urgent.

Women do not make boys into men. While I raise my hat at their valuable attempts to do this, unfortunately, they make them into their female images of how they want males to behave. The boys then remain in their mothers' grips. The result is that they often remain passive, with effeminate qualities. Their male energy stays imprisoned and underdeveloped. Men have needs and instincts distinctly different from women. As I stated earlier in my book, men make men.

Males—especially young men whose tasks are to sort out who they are and where they want to go—need guidance from adult and mature men. Because mothers tend to give unconditional love, they do not provide young men the necessary limits that mature men can give to the impulsive tendencies of younger males. The limits and direction that mature men teach young men give them permission to channel their energy toward positive and constructive outlets, instead of falling into chaotic behavior.

Advice Is Not Enough

Without strong and focused desire, advice is not worth a damn. As an educational psychologist, I can attest to this. Parents, doctors, teachers, wise elders, and intelligent watchers of the political scene say the same. Convincing evidence of this intractable trait of the human race is the result of thousands of diet books and $45 billion a year touted to weight-loss devices. Yet Americans are fatter than ever. The brutal fact is that information without disciplined action does not work, for disciplined action *is* work.

> *For in everything that we do the body is useful; and in all uses of the body it is of great importance to be in as high a state of physical fitness as possible.*
> —Socrates

The body is the fundamental basis for everything. It is where you live 24/7. Kids in the 21st century do not understand the long-term payoff of years of consistency and persistence to master skills. They are an entire generation of "now, quick, give it to me in a second" people, and they are programmed for immediate rewards. This is highly unfortunate for their futures.

However, the good news is that by taking action (which requires discipline and regular practice), they will earn the results they need. A couple of tries will *not* do the job. Focusing steadily on goals daily and weekly over a period of time will bring results. Defined muscles do not happen with one or two tries at the gym. Form shows up after months of exercise. So it is with every other worthy skill and plan, including the actions suggested in this guide. Focusing steadily is the important behavior.

The number of hours one spends working is not the best measure for reaching one's goals. It is the quality and consistency of hours given to learning that counts and gets more efficient results. The results of the test show when the desired effects of your effort begin to appear; this is proof that you are on the right track.

Do What Works for You

The actions suggested here are not formulas or medical prescriptions. They are given as basic tools and skills to help you navigate smoothly through the demanding stuff life throws at you. The point I wish to convey is that failure is a learning experience, and you may move through many cycles before you learn what you need in order to make it work and before they've served their purposes.

The 21st century is in its adolescence; it is ever evolving and changing at a very rapid pace. Much like humans, its character is being formed. The rules of the game of this century are in a starting position and in an adjustment phase.

Failure and frustration are inevitable components of this change. Don't be too frustrated; simply grasp what you need, and move on to something that works better.

The best anyone can do during these rapidly changing times is to hold on to fundamentals. Be acutely alert of the economic, social, and political shifts around you, and guard against the traps set up to pick your pocket and your life's energy. A young man will gain immeasurable benefits when he puts forth the effort to learn, read, and explore what is around him. Be ready and awake.

To make it easier to guide you through this morass, growth, and uncertainty, seeking a respectable adult role model could significantly help.

Benefits of Higher Standards

Since the beginning of time, men have been expendable. The strong will eat the weak. Looking and learning about the faults and shortcomings of any society, especially in the rapidly changing one we are swimming in now, will give you an edge in the long run. The reason is that social systems, including numbers of corporations and individuals, are geared to exploit. This situation is especially true for the male gender, because past and present cultures have chewed up men for their own purposes. This includes moving up the corporate ladder, sacrifices in wars, and involvement in many work situations, from blue to white collar.

When both sides of your brain are working together and your emotional, social, and aesthetic sensitivities are educated, you are less likely to get chewed up and spit out. And when your work skills are well honed, it gives you even more defenses.

When these important parts of you are coherent, strength and resilience come about. In the face of adversity and challenges, you will be better able to withstand the stress.

It is about being unified. When the parts of yourself are united, you are stronger. Your strength gets scattered when parts are divided. This is true for nations, groups, families, individuals, and businesses. Having long-range goals provides purpose and vision, which fuel the strength to endure. Understanding the major challenges, needs, and benefits of the cycles in your life fortifies against self-imposed setbacks and losses. The more you know about yourself and how to adapt to the learning opportunities around you, the better equipped you are to succeed and to live well, longer, and healthier.

What Serves You and What Screws You

Challenging the values of the times and milieu (surroundings) in which you must live and hopefully flourish does not mean rejecting them. It means that understanding the favored thinking, the laws, and the types of people in your environment can serve you, or it can screw you up.

As a unique person with individual needs that are special only to you, you should know the ins and outs of society's values and demands. This will help you realize what serves you or hinders your progress. I cannot emphasize this enough: *do not* pay attention to what the media peddles to the masses and followers. Remember, you're working on being a leader. Discern what you see, hear, and think and what others are telling you. Also work on getting to know the opportunities around you, particularly those that move you along or hold you back in your current setting. Know what you know, but know what you don't know, too.

Lastly, you especially need to be alert to the economic state of things, which can either pick your pocket or fill it. Doing this requires questioning, fact finding, and thinking. It is not a task for the mediocre. Don't follow "that guy," who jumps into what is happening now. Be the young man who chooses to be complete and develop into a successful man, who has both the left and right sides of his brain in gear and who is tuned in to feelings and emotions—both his and those around him. And work hard on creating a long-range economic plan that will take you well into your eightieth year. Above all, seek a high and energizing purpose and ambition for a successful and full adult life.

J.D. Lee

Where did I come from? Who am I? Where am I going?

THE CORE OF MANHOOD: FATHER, SEXUALITY, AND WORK

The Male's Silent Hunger for the Father

In *Adam's Return,* Richard Rohr writes:

> Much of the human race experiences an immense father hunger. It is felt by women, but even so by men. It seems that same-sex parent has a unique importance in a child's life, and his or her absence leaves huge, aching hole inside that is never really filled...I have found it to be the single most prevalent absence in the human soul, and also one of the most painful. But the pain is quiet, hidden, denied and takes many shapes and forms that sons cannot care or to grasp.

Rohr certainly hit the nail on the head with that quote. "Father hunger" refers to the need for a father figure. Unfortunately, it is not a topic that young men feel comfortable talking about. As a norm, they are either incapable or are reluctant, for various reasons, to acknowledge this situation. It begins with the reluctance of older men to take on the roles of mature father figures, thereby creating a lack of clarity in instructing young men to manhood. These are only some of the reasons why this deeply emotionally loaded topic stays locked up inside men's psyches. As a result, the connected, potent masculine energy becomes scattered and often misplaced to destructive and self-defeating aims. In an ideal situation, the father provides a model for a young male to accept authority, guidance, and limits. When these fundamentals are absent, trouble brews.

Delinquent Elephants

Would you believe that the lack of an adult-male animal in a herd affects the animal world as much as the lack of a father figure to a young man? Young male elephants in Africa, Thailand, and India have been reported stamping out villages, stomping on Volkswagens, and killing young elephants and even humans who crossed their paths. These adolescent elephants had broken away from their natural adjustments within the herd. The scientists and rangers observed that no mature bull elephants were present in each of these herds because most had been poached for their ivory. So the adolescent male elephants roamed about the country in unsupervised gangs. After the rangers introduced the bull elephants into the herds again, the once-delinquent elephants adjusted to the herds and, in a few weeks, began to behave normally once more. The lack of adult males and the presence of unsupervised young males are the two major variables in the equation that equal delinquent behavior.

Eighty-five percent of youths in prison have absent fathers, and 90 percent of all inmates in prison are men. Rohr, the Franciscan priest quoted in the beginning of this chapter, served for many years as a chaplain in a New Mexico prison. He reported that nearly all the male inmates had either not known their fathers or had no significant relationships with them.

Male youths without fathers behave like fatherless elephants.

The book *War Against Boys* outlines a study of six thousand boys from the ages of fourteen to twenty-nine; it showed that fatherless boys were twice as likely to be jailed than boys whose fathers were present. The link between having no fathers and violence among young men is so powerful that it overrides the impact of race, economic status, and educational level of the parents.

These facts usurp all the hoopla about the unfairness of race, money, and educational levels. The basic problem influencing young men's bad behavior is the absence of fathers. Without an effective father, a meaningful elder, or an active father figure, a young male has two strikes against him. He is far more likely to get into trouble and to make trouble than a young male who has an elder to guide him.

Young females aren't immune from the absence of their fathers' influences, either. A fatherless home greatly increases a teenage girl's probability of becoming pregnant, of falling victim to sexual exploitation, and, later in life, of experiencing relationship instability with men. Conversely, the father presence benefits both genders.

What Happens to the Male's Psyche When the Father Is Not Around?

Without a father or active model of a father, a young male flops around, grasping for someone or some deed to validate him as a man. An absent father opens a hole in a young man's psyche. If the father or significant elder does not fill in the young man's need for a male role model, then the mother does. Then, he falls into the mother's control in one way or another and becomes a mama's boy.

No male worthy of manhood wants this. If he becomes personally aware of this state of affairs distorting his masculine growth, he would spin around 180 degrees in the opposite direction. But most men in their developing stages are not aware of this crippling dynamic. Nevertheless, unconsciously, the innate instinctual drive to be masculine pushes a male to seek some proof that he is not in mama's arms and is definitely not a girl. If he fails to overcome some difficult challenge or does not gain recognition by men that he has succeeded in the challenge, then he tends to seek validation as a man in counterfeit devices that cover up his unrecognized insecurities of being a man. Many of these cover-ups are superficial, low in power, and provide little, if any, strength, insight, or support for independence.

They include a wide range of exaggerated images of masculinity, such as unkempt appearance, disinterest in dress, vulgar and loud language, lack of good manners and social skills, and avoidance of personal feelings and not talking about them. They also include owning power objects, such as high-octane cars, screaming motorcycles, and other things that clearly mark males; these are distinct from what girls are supposed to do, have, or look like, and they give them false senses of power and control.

Then there are the destructive compensations for the deeply buried want to be affirmed as a man. Gangs are substitutes for male authority. They have established members who assume authority; they have rites of initiation and activities that affirm power and respect, which, sadly, are often illegal. Yet the gangs hold on because they provide a means of validating males.

They choose this way of life because they weren't aware of the alternative, acceptable, and constructive ways of making a male affirm himself as a man. They simply weren't in their environments. Behaviors of violence and criminal activities often give feelings of power and strength to the people committing them. According to the gender count in jails, men have a 97 percent monopoly of these on self-defeating behaviors. The telling link is that most of the men in jails lack significant relationships with their fathers. Anger gnaws at their insides, festering from the betrayal of having no fathering of the masculine self.

THE WAY TO MANHOOD

Step One: Fathering Yourself

There is an awesome commercial out there: "Friends don't let friends drink and drive." Well, I also have a recommendation: "Friends don't ask friends to father them." They are unlikely to know any more than you do, anyway. Moreover, about half of them either grew up without a father or didn't have great father figures. An indication of this is that about 50 percent of the households in the United States are headed by single mothers. Consequently, about half of the young-adult men in the country are searching for role models to aspire to. With or without a father (especially an emotionally distant father) a young male needs to father himself. How? By forming an image of a mature and admirable man to aspire to be like. It does not mean copying or imitating that person. It means choosing the qualities and habits that serve your unique self.

Step Two: Fathering Yourself If Your Father Is Around

You are a lucky young man who probably has a basic male identity. However, you do not have your father's characteristics, abilities, or faults. Those are all uniquely his. You are a separate individual with your own personality, characteristics, and abilities. Most surely have faults. The benefit of having a father around is that he set limits and provides energy and strength to help guide his son's ambitions. But it is up to the son to strive toward his goals and succeed, by seeking qualities in admirable males that match his individual needs and abilities.

The task given to young men is to select hero figures who can father them. We are going to call them "father-heroes." These praiseworthy men can be living or dead and can have overcome significant obstacles to achieve something you want to achieve.

I am an example of this process. I stuttered horribly as a young man, and it was very embarrassing. Though my father didn't have this issue, he was supportive. Even with that, I felt it important to seek guidance from someone who had the same issues so that I could be rid of this terrible hindrance. I read that Demosthenes (383–322 BC), one of the great orators of ancient Greece, conquered his stuttering by putting pebbles in his mouth while practicing speeches. I did the same for a while and chose marbles.

The technique seemed to help me. At least I no longer stuttered chronically. Working and practicing with Herculean effort, I overcame my disability, thereby embarrassing the professional doubters who held the belief that I would stutter for life. By taking initiative and finding that great achiever who had experienced the same issue, I was victorious. To this day, I believe that I won because this was imprinted in the back of my mind: "If Demosthenes overcame his stuttering and made history by a strong effort, so can I." Even though the story is two millennia old, he nevertheless served as an active father-hero for me. It worked.

As a 21st century young man, you should seek out your father-hero.

Step Three: Fathering Yourself If Your Father Is Absent
Not having a father around may tend to cause issues, such as lack of confidence, inability to set limits and focus, and lack of direction. Some may be lucky enough to have a father figure, such as an uncle, teacher, neighbor, or coach. Unfortunately,

they will lack the biological blood connection that truly bonds a father and son, so what is to be done in that case?

You must choose to father yourself with deliberate and consistent effort. This is a big job; but done reasonably well, a young man can become a man's man. Making the conscious and very intelligent choice to father yourself is a major yet beneficial decision.

The next challenge is to decide which kind of father figure, man, or elder male to use as your model. As stated above, you should seek out a father-hero. In the 21st century, we are facing challenges in finding worthy male models. Pop culture and instant gratification have truly become hindrances. The images of males the media projects on TV, films, and other electronic devices usually lack depth, integrity, and wisdom. And more often than not, they are badly behaved, and the people they portray do not represent the truth. These men are products with artificial faces designed to promote sales and generate money. Although some are accomplished in sports, business, and other skills, their over-the-top achievements are out of reach for 99 percent of everyone else.

The positive aspect of the media, if sought out by the millennial youth, does have men with great achievements. There are networks dedicated to science and scientific breakthroughs, learning about men of insight and literary excellence and men who uplift quality of life. Seeking out men whom you can respect and setting achievements within the limits of your capabilities will garner greater results in the long run. Batman is great, but don't jump off any buildings. Again, find your real father-hero.

Step Four: Taking Action

We've said a lot in this chapter, and now it's time to take action.

A direct way of fathering yourself is to develop an image of the man you wish to mature into. One of the primary ways to accomplish this is to seek out older, more mature men you admire, who embody the characteristic traits you wish to emulate and achievements you wish to attain. These men always carry knowledge that can help you turn your life in the right direction.

This is something all young men need to keep in mind. There is negative identification as well. You can also learn something from men whom you do not admire and/or men in your direct environment. They present faults, such as beer bellies, unhealthy living, compulsive drinking, and uncontrolled tempers, lack of discipline, intractable stubbornness, and other undesirable traits and behaviors that you do not want to copy. You must say to yourself, "I do not want to be like that. These men went the wrong way. Not for me. I am better than that." Head in the opposite direction, and seek out the father-hero we've discussed. He is out there.

Strive to develop habits that produce positive results from men you admire and have personal contact with as well as heroic men of the past. Take and learn their methods of success, and work to make them part of your daily existence. Find people who pull you up, not drag you down. Self-fathering will enable so much in your life.

A well accomplished musician I knew summed up the message in different words: "You may not be a genius, but hang around musicians a cut above you. Inevitably, you'll learn a lot, then work to be better."

THE BENEFITS OF A MENTOR

A mentor has knowledge of and experience with his profession and skills. He is successful in his chosen field of work. He does more than just teach his understudy. A mentor takes a personal, one-to-one interest in training and guiding the apprentice in his care.

Any young man who can latch onto a mentor in whatever capacity, whether in investing, acting, welding, construction, management, medicine, computer programming, sports, and so on, has an enormous advantage to succeed. He is a very lucky young man, indeed, because the mentor provides knowledge that only experience can give. Equally important, a mentor provides an identity and adult role model. A mentor is not likely to seek you out. A young man needs to draw upon his store of male energy to aggressively search and persuade a mentor to take him on. Passion speaks volumes when knowledge isn't quite there.

Finding a Mentor

There are many adult men who are successful in their chosen lines of work who know considerably more than you. These men of worth can be fathers, uncles, neighbors, teachers, or employers. Fraternal organizations, sports, and some male-based interest groups have men available to serve as guides for young men. Most are more than willing to help, give advice, and support your goals. But you need to search and ask. Most importantly, you need to research the line of work, nature of the business, and the company and/or person with whom you are seeking to work and grow.

If you do not show focused interest in what you want, no one else will be interested in you, either. Use the following magic words: "I've researched you and the company and feel I would be a great fit for you"; "I am interested in working with you and your company; I will start at any level to grow within your organization"; "I read you're looking for x, and I am best suited for that position."

First impressions are very important, and proper attire goes a long way. Be well groomed, and dress cleanly with clothes that fit and are tasteful. Respect is the first gesture you must give to a potential mentor and/or employer.

THE SEXES: THE MALE AND FEMALE GENDERS

I edited my book to avoid crucifixion by the sex know-it-all crowds, because many views in this chapter are not in the popular curriculum of boy-girl behavior. You will be presented with alternative outlooks on ways to come to terms with the complex sex and sexual identity issues. These views could cause anger in people with set opinions on these matters. They can also clear out confusion and anxiety about basic sexual issues in this time of tolerant sexual experimentation.

    A young man can use his good intelligence to look between the lines and seek truths in hidden places. If he puts forth diligent effort to explore the latter suggestion, he can very possibly uncover truths about sex, sexuality, and gender identity that cannot be printed here. This chapter was created because many young men are feminized, if not consciously, then unconsciously. We are going to explore this.

Male, Female: Opposites or Both?

The phallus is deemed by young men, older men, and all men to be godlike in its power. It is a vital and creative energy of great force. Its penetrating power causes it to be worshipped in various ways, both symbolically and intimately, in all cultures, past and present. The fact is that, though the male has the phallus, which defines his maleness, the biological setup has orchestrated the male with an X female chromosome and a Y male chromosome. There isn't a vitamin to rid you of this setup.

The tender baby with the dangling participle comes out of the womb with the two genetic dispositions stated above. The female, on the other hand, has two X chromosomes. It would seem then, just from the basic biology, that the male has a tremendous amount of options in his sexuality.

He has both genders under his skin. Sexual identity goes beyond hormones and genes. The causes are complicated. They include childhood experiences, personal interactions, social and cultural values, education, and freedom of expression. Moreover, sexual identity and sexuality is fluid and changeable and is even deemed fashionable. Yes, you read that correctly. It shifts with the times and many cultures. Whether you're white, black, brown, or green, or whether you have declared yourself male or female, no one on this planet is exclusively one or the other.

Sexual identity is not defined by physical contact alone or by a desire for the same or the opposite sex. Masculine, feminine, same, and opposite sexual identities include emotional, mental, and cultural values, which are defined as acceptable and valued in many societies. An era can depict what is acceptable or unacceptable behavior in one society or another. While it could be deemed a sin to some, in another cultural group or time, it is quite normal.

A case in point occurs with the word "homosexual." It was invented in the nineteenth century and came into use in 1892 in the English translation of Krafft-Ebing's book *Psychopathia Sexualis*. A male or a female can be erotically attracted to beauty in either sex, regardless of gender. The ancients (Greeks, Romans, and other cultures) and some modern societies were—and are—far more in tune with their baser instincts and indulged without judgment, unlike today's modern Western man. While they had very open attitudes toward gender identity regarding with whom they indulged erotically, *we* are trained to believe that "this, this, and this" makes "this, this, and this," and you had better not veer too far from society's "this and that." Oh, the judgments we are trained to believe and carry in our minds!

Even today, there are societies with large populations that carry attitudes that favor the beauty of the person, rather than gender, as the mark of erotic attraction. This natural tendency applies, especially for young adults who are in their processes of sorting out who they are during their experimenting stages. Consequently, there should be no fear or anxiety about same-sex or opposite-sex sexual attraction.

The issue is acting on that attraction prematurely. Peer pressure and giving into the fashionable thing to do often causes trouble. Fortunately, insecurities and confusion eventually subside as emotional, intellectual, and social maturity inevitably grows. Whom you are attracted to will very likely take its proper direction as you develop. The answer and decision of your persuasions are yours. The direction you choose is yours alone.

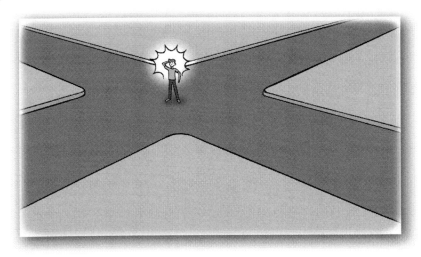

As an educational psychologist, I've dealt a great deal with this topic. It is not easy for anyone to face his or her family and peers with a decision that defies societal norms. It is personal and individual because the variables that cause sexual identity are far too complex for anyone outside of oneself to judge. The task is to live that choice well, intelligently, and in good taste.

Sex: The Act! (It Gets better as You Get Older)
Sex gets better as you get older? For men in their twenties and even younger, this may sound like a lie or a propaganda statement from a Planned Parenthood group. It is not. Many mature

men, including myself, who have been around the block and who have the experience and perspective of time, can affirm positively that this is sound advice. Sex, the act, gets better as you get older. This is especially good advice for young men who are ambitious. What they don't grasp is that sex is a powerful deflector of energy that can consequently trip them up. My advice is to take it easy on yourself. It's not a marathon. With time and maturity, it's much more satisfying and rewarding.

Try to focus on school and career goals—especially as a young man in your twenties through your early thirties—without letting sex and romantic relations interfere with attaining them. You will be very pleased and surprised by the type of wonderful relationships you can build once life isn't complicated with all the other aspects of accomplishments on your path.

Taking Action

Young men and women currently in their twenties often lack the social and emotional communication skills needed to make contact with each other. They feel anxiety, friction, and the dumpy feeling that goes along with the suspicion of being judged and rejected. Even history and ancient times have noted that it takes time to learn about the ways in which males and females connect with each other. That hasn't changed, although the Internet influences a false sense of confidence.

Unfortunately, the complexity and social diversity of this century seems to be delaying the learning processes. Social media has created the false reality of social interaction and has encouraged emotional isolation. It has also allowed rude, inappropriate, and vulgar language without the reprimands that any normal person and social interaction would allow. While it certainly has expanded our reaches, it has done very little to encourage friendly, one-on-one experience. Now, we have a lot of media-bound young men and women with false senses of reality. When they enter the real world, well, there are crickets. The big question is: "What can men do to remove the feeling of being clumsy and awkward around women?"

Overcoming Being Shy

One thing all young men have in common, inevitably, is the first experience of feeling shy around girls—especially ones they "like," even though they may not realize it at those moments. Then come the times to meet and actually speak to them. Often at a loss for words, boys trying to fish for a conversation starter are uncomfortable. Though many of these young men are in their teens, not much changes for many men in their early twenties; they often find themselves still awkward.

Nobody wants to look like a jerk. Sooner or later, all men do. Everyone makes mistakes, and being rejected is just part of the game. Both genders, well into their twenties and beyond, are still learning how to relate to the opposite sex. They are unsure and insecure in their approaches. For young women, the insecurity is much less, as they are socially more advanced and sensitive to feelings than their male counterparts. Consequently, they are capable of pulling the strings when it comes men's emotions and have the manipulative skills to be in control. Young men sense this, recognized or not, and almost always fear it.

The superior social awareness, coupled with both genders learning how to engage one another, considerably increases the odds of clumsy and painful social mistakes. It puts the less socially aware male in the unenviable position of being misunderstood and rejected.

The rapid changes happening now in the 21st century are also contributing to confused communication between the sexes. Social roles and sexual identities have been coming apart and are still being tested. Consequently, the new clashes with the old, and the conflict sets girls and boys wondering how to adjust to the latest rules of the game. As a result, neither sex really understands what is going on between them. The major concern about misunderstood communication can lead to mistaken accusations of sexual harassment in all areas of young men's lives.

While I give many solutions in this chapter, the greatest advice I can say about ridding oneself of the fear of communication is this: get out from behind that computer, and begin interacting more on a personal level with real flesh-and-blood women. As with anything in life, practice will always make perfect. If things are not perfect, at least there will be improvement.

Improving Understanding

Who doesn't want to improve his or her understanding skills? Well, young men, mostly. Once they leave their homes, they tend to be a bit resistant for some time. First, let's talk about learning the cues to make graceful ins and smooth exits, and we'll learn the social lubricants of getting to know people. It takes practice. This is true in all aspects of one's life, whether one is at work, with friends, or with the opposite sex. It has to be done with real people who are close enough to touch. Why? Because the core of getting to know someone on a meaningful level comes from the numerous nonverbal messages, feeling tones, and subtle and subconscious cues the physical body beams out. In this age of digital media, it is critical to keep in mind that images blasted on digital screens block out most of these basic, human-to-human, physical channels of communication. It is like the difference between seeing a picture of a luscious hamburger or smelling, craving, and eating it. Yum! The gap between communicating with women on your computer screen versus sitting down to lunch with them is just as great as this example implies. Let's pull her out of the screen.

Secondly, a young man can examine how shy he may feel because he has placed himself in a real-life scenario. Every man has feelings about being awkward around women, even though he wants to show competency, muscle, and I-am-great bravado. Unfortunately, it does not cover up the underlying fears of being embarrassed.

So you study and learn about the differences in the languages of females and males by being present, paying attention, listening, and learning from mistakes and any embarrassing messages. You learn to read these messages by interacting with the opposite sex and by studying the behavior of their female natures. The good news is that it is a basic law that doing it consistently brings rewards, including overcoming shyness and well-earned self-confidence.

When She Catches Your Eye

For decades, I have worked with young men in helping them overcome their shyness. I promise that it may be tough, but you won't die trying, though at times, it may feel that way. Here are some tips.

Say "Hello" to her. If she seems receptive, you can follow up with a number of responses:

"My name is——"

"What are you doing sitting here all alone? May I join you?"

Referring to something interesting about her dress is usually a winner: "I love your shoes/dress/hair."

"What does the design on your necklace mean?" Certainly, you can assess the situation, as there may be other openers that would encourage her to talk before your shyness backs you off. Listen, and say little as you gage her interest and assess your interest as well. You do not have to do much more than that. Almost everyone, especially the female gender, is pleased by an attentive audience.

"How is your day going so far?"

If she's reading a business magazine or *The Wall Street Journal*, try, "How do you feel about our current economic situation?" Look natural and smile, just enough to show that you're pleased to be around her, talking with her, and hearing what she has to say.

When the conversation is over, you can end with gauging the level of interest and/or her reticence. You can always ask for her phone number. If she is apprehensive, ask her for her social media information, and tell her that you would like to get to know her. Be polite and attentive. Leave it with this: "Nice talking with you. A pleasure to meet you."

If you feel that more can happen, give her a card that has your name, e-mail address, and something interesting about yourself printed on it. Your business card would certainly be impressive. Have those readily available; they are easy and inexpensive.

I want to leave off with the adage that "practice makes perfect." You can be very hopeful about all of this because as you mature and work on overcoming your shyness, confidence will surely follow.

Rejection Is Part of the Game

Don't be put off by the title of this chapter, especially since we just covered how to overcome shyness and catch her eye. Rejection is part of the game, and we're going to walk through this together. Females, as almost all warm-blooded animals, are biologically wired to attract. And men are wired to pursue.

Nature created it; culture has reinforced this. Men make the advances, and women receive or reject them. You, as a male, are wired to make advances and to take action: call her, ask her out, pay for dinner, call again, buy some stuff, ask her out again, make the moves, build a relationship, make a commitment, and the final one—offer an invitation to marry. If it doesn't sound exhausting, it actually can be fun.

Inevitably, in the dating cycle and fun, you will get a goodbye, and a breakup will happen. You may or may not have seen it coming. Undoubtedly, you may feel humiliated, and certainly, the ego will be bruised and hurt. All of these are normal feelings that go along with her pushing you away. Don't feel too bad because, even in nature, leopards miss capturing their prey six out of seven times.

Makeups and breakups are inevitable, so grasp the boy-girl language. Generally, you will learn it through the school of hard knocks, and it is unavoidable. How can you reduce the number of mistakes and disappointments? Most importantly, work on making yourself a complete, well-rounded, and balanced man who makes it a priority to learn the art of living well. Classy women admire and would never look down on a man who has manners, dresses cleanly, acts confidently, and speaks with intelligence.

Acquire a skill or a job you can master. Every man can do this. The key is to find an occupation that you desire and have a natural ability to do. Be patient. You will be in charge because an unmarried man over the age of thirty who has put himself together is independent and has the spirit to enjoy living; he then becomes high-end bait for the right type of woman. It is a game changer. You will be the prey and the hunted one, thereby giving you more choices.

DECODING THE FEMALE: BASICS FOR THE MALE

Her "Yes" and Her "No"

Males, from early puberty and as long as their hormones flow, explore, roam, and seek the hunt. Their biological ancestry predisposes them to make the first move, particularly when the females are predisposed to welcome their advances. The challenge for the male making the move is the female's power to permit or stop the motion. She may say "yes," or she may say "no." Consider a female dog in heat. Every male dog in the neighborhood gets the scent and jumps the fence for the bitch's favors. But she accepts only one male out of the bunch. This occurred in my large backyard several years ago.

Six male dogs jumped a five-foot fence to get at my sweet Queeny. She snarled and snapped at the suitors she did not want to receive. Her "no" was unambiguous. She chose only one—the alpha of the pack, a German shepherd.

Men aren't so different from dogs. It's instinctual for men to seek, choose and mate, which parallels the young male's testosterone-driven urge and cultural wiring to make the first advances to the female. He does this almost unconsciously, having hardly a clue on how to approach the available female, much less how to encourage her socially or sexually.

Throughout adolescence and the early-adult period, the developing male usually learns the hard way by trial and error, receiving embarrassing "nos" in varying degrees and some grateful "yeses" for his effort. Keep in mind that most women mature faster and have filters that have standards for acceptance and rejection. When compared to a male of her age, a female is generally more socially adept, and she may smile to herself while thinking of how the male is not quite up to her standards. At first, he may be that rejected dog that jumped the fence. Fortunately, in time, most young men eventually gain inner strength to control themselves appropriately and learn when and what to say and when not to say anything at all. At first, women are normally disposed to say "no" indirectly. This applies more for younger women who don't have a lot of dating experience. Keep that in mind if you are a young man yourself, wading in the dating pool. However, you're less likely to get a "no" if you are keeper material and suited for her. You'll feel the connection.

At the same time, keep in mind, and discern wisely, that when she says "no" directly or in its variations, she means "no," and you should go away. Learn to make a distinction between the absolute "no" and the conditional or ambiguous "no." Men are also predisposed to pursue. If you feel that she is shy, reserved, and not able to communicate her feelings, a gentler approach to getting the "yes" drawn out of her is by getting her to open up and talk about herself. This is a much easier way to assess her personality. Don't forget that just because you jump the fence, it doesn't always mean that you need to hump the bitch. Feel out the situation, and respond accordingly.

She's Not Lying

To say that a woman's emotions are complex is the understatement of the century. While men tend to be steadier and more even-tempered on the whole, women can be emotional yo-yos. Any man who's even remotely entered into the dating pool will understand this.

In speaking "her truth," a female expresses what she feels at the very moment she is saying it. But feelings are fickle. They change and go up, down, and sideways. One second, she's an angel, sprouting wings, and the very next, she is like

Medusa, with snakes shooting out of her head. She might say no and then say yes to the same issue ten minutes later. Her feelings have changed. She is just expressing that change, and she has the right to do so. She is not lying.

Let's take asking a woman out on a date as an example of how women's emotions play a part. Whatever a man's intentions are—to take her to dinner or to become friendlier—a woman expects a man to persist if he is sincerely interested in her. Ladies who have a lot of self-respect will not jump to a quick yes when asked out. So an interested man keeps asking, while she keeps feeding him cues to make him doubt her interest in him. This is an ageless and archetypal pattern of how men and women interact.

He is testing the strength of his desire for her. During this starting period, she is probably not sure whether she wants him or not. The man, as well, may be uncertain of his feelings for the woman. She may wonder, "Is he just flirting, giving me attention without intention?" "What is he after?" "Do I really like him?" "Do I want to date him?" "Is he just for fun or marriage material?" Yes, they can think all of those things in a span of two minutes.

Waffling and uncertain, she wants the man to persist in courting her until she can make up her mind. As I stated in the previous chapter, every situation or environment may be different; the man will need to assess her body language versus her answer. She may be putting out a "no" vibe, but she is very interested in interacting, and the rapport is there. So if the situation brings about a no when you ask her out, but the energy contradicts the answer, then figure out a polite, respectful, and courteous way to change her mind by pursing her. Remember, she is not lying, but she may change her mind down the road.

When a "No" Can Be Dangerous

Being young certainly has its advantages and disadvantages. I wrote *The Man You Can Be For The 21st Century* because I wanted to bring my insights and expertise to young men. This conversation we are about to have is cogent, especially today. We've explored "She's Not Lying," so how does a man learn to read the nuances of the "nos" correctly? It's a shame that in some instances, being persistent and making advances could cause a petulant and insecure female to charge a young man, who is rather naive in his understanding of women, with sexual harassment, thereby ruining his life. This can and does happen in various situations in social events, at work, and especially on college campuses, whether the charges are substantiated or unsubstantiated.

How about the other way around, when a female advances? Females can be inappropriate by being sexually aggressive, too, although they are usually less direct. This situation of reading the "yeses" and "nos" becomes more difficult when the woman in not clearly attuned to her feelings or gives misleading cues to the male.

One saying that tickles me is this: "Women are like spaghetti. They tend to tangle their feelings in a bunch and struggle to unravel them." Though that is a fun saying, it holds an indelible truth. How? A woman's mood can change in accordance with her likes and dislikes of men's interest in her. So the result can be that neither of them adequately understand each other and misinterpret the cues that enable each of them to relate to each other appropriately.

This is why it is essential, as a maturing man, to build a firm foundation of masculinity (strength, endurance, purpose, and understanding) and be fully attuned to what is happening around you. *Pay attention!* It's important to know what you know and know what you don't know. If you aren't sure about the attention and where the conversation is leading, then don't make any moves.

Once confidence and knowledge is gained, you will have the delightful delight of delighting in women.

The Female: Basics Every Man Should Know

Fantasy #1

A young woman's first want and primary fantasy, ingrained by biology, conditioned by nature and still active in the female, liberated culture of today, is marriage. Don't let this sentence scare you. Being *The Man You Can Be For The 21st Century* means being in tune and aware of females at every age. Eventually, you will be at an age and in a place where you will fall love and desire the same. But let's get back to her.

She's not going to marry any man off the street. Young women will seek out men who provide sufficient cash flow to give them options, without their having to worry about money. These options may include being able to work in a career that pleases her, or perhaps having the ability to work less while having children, or having a family without having to work at all, thanks to sufficient funds coming from hubby.

The bottom line is this: if you want to meet and marry your desired mate in life, be ready. Whether she wants to be a rocket scientist, own her own business, or be an artist with a modest income, you're ready. You will be the consummate provider.

The number one fantasy and drive for women is to marry and have economic security. The demands of child rearing have structured the roles of mother and father, homemaker and breadwinner. Women have also set up other criteria for men to match: be attractive (take care of himself), show respect, be healthy, be emotionally available, have some brains, be single, and be successful (or on the road to success).

The point for the young, unmarried man to keep in mind is that the unmarried woman will view him as the eligible male with the intent of auditioning him for her primary fantasy, marriage. If she is serious in her intent toward him, she will act cautiously because she is still tallying up his goods. So let's make sure you got the goods!

Fantasy #2
The problem with the stable, good earner whose energy is sapped by long working hours is that he is not exciting or passionate and does not provide variety.

He no longer sweeps her off her feet, gives her undivided attention, courts her romantically, showers her with gifts, takes her on exotic vacations, or provides bell-ringing sex. Simply put, he is overworked, tired, stressed out, and on his way to becoming boring. Unless the girlfriend/wife can freelance around or perform hubby switching, she may resort to female forms of pornography.

While men watch straight-on porn, most women find it in romance novels, although most will not admit it. They will keep their fantasy/sex secrets from men. They are too smart, too realistic, or too respectful to cuckold the boyfriend/husband.

The reason women read these novels is that they wish to live vicariously through the heroine and be ravished by a handsome prince, who is adoring and exciting and who provides glamour and romance. He also gives her an opportunity to have a starring role in something requiring little effort on her part. While some women rarely admit to having these sexual fantasies, billions of dollars in romance-novel sales say differently. If they were honestly candid about their secret sexual desires, they would put themselves on view to be judged as loose and openly sexual, which is a no-no for society's image of what "good girls" should be.

The point is that both married and unmarried women will look at the men with the intention of seducing them to perform their secondary fantasies. The danger is that men won't be able to recognize whether females want them for hubby or bubbly, or both. Women are very good at the sex appeal game and at sending mixed messages. Whether he is in the flirting stage, the dating game, or a marriage, and especially in intimate encounters, the man should have some clues regarding how the game is played.

THE 21ST CENTURY WOMAN AND YOU: SEARCHING AND INDEPENDENT

Fantasies #1 and #2 reflect the needs built into females' DNA. They have been shaped by biology and culture and drive their sexuality with no less force than the phallic and masculine energy that impels male sexuality.

But because women today strive for economic and social independence, the long hours of homework required to learn a paying skill often force them to delay fulfilling the instincts that drive their feminine natures. This presents a problem for the young-adult female as well as for the young-adult male. Mating and sexual desires do not go away because you are in school and ambitious for a career.

For young women, whose biology is timed, the conflict between delaying basic instincts and realizing them causes greater dilemmas than for the males. Males can wait awhile, but females have schedules.

Women Today Have Many Options

Today's young woman has many more options in her life to sort out than in past years. Her choices over the years have vastly expanded: she can choose to get married and have her husband be the primary moneymaker or be married and have a career at the same time. She can remain single and live with a man. She can choose to have children or not or even to have more than one child, with or without a husband in the home. A big option recently is single mothers having babies by donors. Or a woman may opt to go the traditional route and have the family, husband, house, and a part-time job and seek a career later in life. Much like men, women have a lot of choices and will need to find what kinds of work, career, and activities suit and energize them.

On the other hand, young men have fewer, more focused goals. They seek first independence, schooling, a job that will hopefully turn into a career. Marriage and family are normally secondary to his purpose. An American woman in the twenty-first century faces many complex and conflicting decisions. It is challenging for many of them to decide what routes to take.

The best advice is to be sensitive to their conflicts, ambiguity, and anxiety about the choices they have to make. Every choice has a price, for both of you. The 21st Century Man needs to mature quicker than ever before to deal with The 21st Century Woman.

Women Today Have a Lot to Offer

Though a young woman may be at odds with herself from all that is thrown at her, she also has a lot to offer a man.

More importantly, with the ever-changing economic circumstances, many young women do not need you for financial support or social advancement. Being a self-assured and independent person in her own right, she can connect with you for who you are rather than the goodies you offer. The man no longer has to be a two-legged ATM to be desirable. His qualities as a maturing man and his character are now in the equation.

So how well put-together are you? Bright, balanced, and educated young women of today will take into account your social, mental, emotional, and career goals. How well integrated are they? What is worthwhile about you? Are you acquainted with the amenities of living—meaning, can you interact with people pleasantly, positively, and without friction? Do women feel at ease around you? Manners carry a young man very far with women and people in general.

A progressive woman wants companionship with a man who is on her level. She is not interested in being bored by a guy who has significant defects in his masculine traits, especially someone whose idea of manliness is backward and outdated. A man of the 21st century is ever forward-looking and holds an expansive masculinity.

The Career Female: You Are Not on Her Shopping List

Some of the 21st century women are focusing on careers and their achievements first and postponing husbands, families, and children. They may put off trying to fulfill these traditionally female roles. These women are not particularly interested in being a Mrs. They are not seeking their identities, worth, and independence in marriage and or in their mate's socioeconomic status, which we discussed earlier.

These women are striving to be people in their own rights. The men in their lives are not their whole lives, like it used to be. Though valuable aspects of their lives, they can live quite well without legal attachments to men. Some career women who seek power tend to put the personal, loving, and committed relationships, which are the functions of the feminine nature, into the deep freezer.

Though a woman may not be aware of this attitude of hers or admit to it, to her, a man is temporarily on hold while she's pursuing other aspirations. This kind of woman is not likely to be vulnerable to your masculine virtues, however handsome, promising, or gifted you may be. This can be somewhat intimidating to a man whose confidence is not on solid ground. So how do you match up to an accomplished and independent young woman? The 21st century young man will work on becoming a complete, accomplished, awake, and mature man in his own right.

Get a firm hold on your deep purpose, and develop your strengths. Learn how to navigate around, through, and within the social, political, and economic conflicts and challenges of the time and the place in which you live.

The Dating Dilemma

Women today want to be treated as equals. But when it comes to dating, the fairer sex wants it the old-fashioned way. Even if she has a good job and income, the woman expects the guy to ask her out and pay in full for the date—hence the dilemma.

49

I have yet to meet a man who claimed that any financially independent woman asked him out, picked him up, paid for the dinner and entertainment, drove him home, and gave him a good-night kiss for the finish. The dating ritual is another example of the conflict between the old, traditional ways and the modern woman, who now has as much independence and financial opportunity as her male counterpart. Chivalry is not dead, gentlemen.

There are far too many circumstances in the dating pool to cover in this book. Suffice it to say that you will need to weigh out each opportunity as it presents itself. If she wants to go dutch on the first date, fine! Be a gentleman, and accept the offer. However, if you're truly interested in a second date and in her, pull out your wallet and old-fashioned values, and insist on taking charge. Plan it, and pay for it. Show her a good time, use your manners, dress to impress, and be on time. Women love men who take action.

At least you know what to do and expect when you date her—that is, if you have the cash!

Boring Men Do Not Please the Modern Female

I've heard quite a few young women complain to me, "Most men I date are boring." I asked them, "Why?" Their responses were that they felt that most men were mentally and emotionally underdeveloped for their ages. They also highly disapproved of men's one-sided conversational focus on work, money, and sports.

The men they met were deficient in their right-brained functions that women are attuned to and that males tend to ignore. Directly put, these men lacked culture, and, even worse, an appreciation for it. The right brain is aesthetically oriented and sees the whole of things. It is also highly intuitive, and young men should learn about this. Not only will it increase the quality of women they wish to attract, but it also heightens their social skills.

Learning about art, music, philosophy, religion, social skills, and other cultures provides perspective and understanding about values worth striving for and how to live them. These studies teach the art of living well and how the world works. The humanities (literature, philosophy, art, religion, music, and so forth) offer an understanding about making life better, regardless of what the world has thrown at us. Accordingly, the modern woman, who struggles on many fronts, cannot help but admire a man who attempts to take up this challenge of learning about the larger, more demanding issues of living well in a complex society.

A friend and doctor whom I greatly admired said, "To be a millionaire and live like one is nothing. But not to have a million and live like one is an art." Work toward your millions, certainly. However, remember that a woman worth having wants her soul nourished.

Taking Action: Manners

"You do not make enemies by being polite." This is a very old and wise saying. Being polite is an infallible social lubricant and draws respectful attention. The problem is that acquiring the skill in polite behavior often presents a challenge, especially in the present culture of sloppy and chaotic informality. By paying attention to mannerly, inoffensive, and pleasing conduct, a young male, whether shy, overly aggressive, or socially obtuse, can avoid the problems of misinterpreting the ambiguities of the female's "yeses" and "nos."

Being Polite: The Basics

Never, never, never touch a woman until she touches you. You will never go wrong obeying this rule. If a girl wants close contact, she will signal it. Just be on alert.

Never, never, never answer a cell phone or make a call in her presence or in the presence of anyone else. It is insulting to do so and is far worse than interrupting someone talking to you.

Always open the car door for a woman. Independent and modern young women often don't expect this. Be different. This gesture gives her respectful attention. Opening the door, pulling out the chair for her when dining out, and standing up when a woman leaves or enters a room are manly courtesies that all women admire. Be a gentleman. It goes a long way.

Always follow through on your appointments and promises. Be on time, but do not expect women to reciprocate. A peculiarity of their gender considers being on time impolite. Be well groomed, and dress appropriately. You know that she will put a lot of time and energy in how she looks.

Learn how to eat slowly and neatly. Do not talk with food in your mouth. Your parents meant that statement to last a lifetime. Sit up straight in your chair. Do not eat with your head bent over the food. Only dogs and cats eat from the bowl on the floor. You're neither. Other details about table manners can be easily researched online. Empower yourself, and read them.

Keep the conversations going. Let her talk more than you. Avoid using "I." People who use "I" excessively in a conversation are guilty of being overly self-concerned and insecure. Instead, ask her about school, work, studies, and her special interests. "What is the hardest thing about your work? Your studies?" "Tell me about your last trip or the book you read." Focus on drawing out thoughts and opinions from her. Be careful about imposing yours and interrupting her.

Don't Presume that she will accept a kiss from you. Extend your hand first and allow her to direct you.

Above All Else praise her with sincere and honest compliments. Search for the feminine qualities of the woman you are with. She carries an abundance of female charms. Many are quiet and hidden underneath her skin, so fish for them and bring them out.

The Man You Can Be For The 21st Century strives to be polished and ready to take on the world.

The Female Nucleus of Inner Being: To Be Loved and Receptive

Hidden and obscured beneath the feminine charms are the trim body, seductive glances, and all the other feminine enticements that attract and keep men. Beneath it all is the desire to be loved. A woman's core of being is to give, receive, and be receptive to love; it fulfills women to the depths of their souls. Nothing substitutes or makes up for the affection and love that men give—not even diamonds rings, pearls, or a BMW. Though many women may cherish those material gifts, the compliments, attention, and love that men show women make them bloom.

The Male Nucleus of Inner Being: To Love, to Achieve, to Give

A man's core of being is action, purpose, achievement, and the ability to love. Men's energy thrusts outward. It is penetrating and is mobilized toward goals. Men thrive by overcoming challenges. When a man who is a man says "yes," he follows through. He does what he says. By keeping his balance, he maintains his strength and focus to carry out his resolve. He does not flake out. Why? Because he knows what he wants, and he knows himself without a doubt. Women admire any man who knows what he wants and goes after it. Such a man can love and can give with strength and attention. Women sense this. When they do, they begin to relax and become receptive.

A young man's sexual instinct can compel him to link his desires with meaningful intentions. Likewise, a young woman's maternal instinct disposes her to perceive him as an enduring mate. However, be aware that hormone-driven affairs fire up the lizard brain, and that it always distorts seeing the real state of things.

Before making any big, life-altering decisions, wait a while, even a few years, until the fire cools and your head clears. There is plenty of time to learn and grow when your masculine energies are intact and not damaged by emotional tornadoes. Remember to think with the big head, not the little one.

THREE REALITIES OF THE 21ST CENTURY IMPACTING MEN TO CHANGE

These realities are 1) the degraded status and condition of men, 2) the increasing dominance and competence of women, and 3) the economic, social, and environmental changes happening now, at the beginning of the 21st century.

These three movements of the 21st century are facts! It's time to wake up and smell the coffee. They will act as punches to the guts for men who are strong enough to confront, challenge, and flourish in spite of them. While some will react strongly, others express considerable concern and are in denial. Though the evidence is painful, a young man on the path to full manhood does not run away. What can be done? A lot! Heed the three points above. The more you know, the more you grow. We'll cover a lot below.

Men's Positions in Modern Society

When the facts are looked at squarely in the eye, they take out large chunks from the male's belief in his self-worth and value.

They point out the modern man's diminished importance and reduced power to control his life and gain independence, financial security, rewarding relationships, health, and self-fulfillment. Though demoralizing, the sum of the data can serve as a kick in the butt to creatively solve what unfairly hinders a young man's progress to independent and valued manhood.

Roy Baumeister wrote the book *Is There Anything Good about Men?* He sums it up here:

> His society may not march him off to death against his will, but it has other uses for him. Its attitude toward him as a man is mixed at best. He will find things subtly stacked against him everywhere, as schools and corporations and other institutions everywhere follow policies officially designed to favor women and girls...He lives in a society that regards women as superior to men, a message echoed everywhere from the private prejudices of individuals to entrenched biases in the legal system, to the news and entertainment media. If he extends the male role by becoming a father, he will find that the avalanche of disrespect gets worse. Furthermore, he will be expected to shoulder a large amount of blame that is not really his.

Measures of Men's Losses of Power

The reaction to depression takes many forms. The high rate of suicide among men flags their loss of power and depression and is the most extreme. *Self-destructive behavior is a prime measure of the inability to control one's life.*

While killing is an aggressive act against someone else, suicide is an aggressive act against oneself when oneself is the enemy. The enemy is not something or someone outside but is internal. The killing of self deems the self as unworthy, unable to change, and powerless. Therefore, the powerless man surrenders and abandons all hope. That which reduces masculine energy includes alcohol, drugs, escapism, compulsive behavior, excessive sexuality, and digital obsession.

Men who energetically seek to find their goals, however, will tap into the essential core of their masculine souls/selves. Everyone has a meaningful purpose, and in some cases, it may be challenging to find what yours is, but "Seek, and ye shall find" is a great saying.

Or as Euripides, an ancient Greek philosopher, said, "Fortune forever fights on the side of the prudent." This means that having sound judgment in practical matters serves your best interests. Also, don't give up. Ever! Even times change, and with hard work, faith, and determination, it will work out. Perseverance wins!

If that's too philosophical for you, try the W. C. Fields quote: "Take the bull by the tail, and face the situation."

Men Commit Suicide Five Times More than Women

* According to American Foundation For Suicide Prevention, men die by suicide 3.5x more often than women. Suicide is the seventh leading cause of death among men and the fourteenth cause of death among women.

* From the ages of ten to fourteen, the boys' rate of suicide is twice the rate of girls in the same age range.
* From the ages of fifteen through nineteen, the male rate of suicide is four times higher than the rate of girls in the same age range.
* From the ages of twenty through twenty-four, the rate of male suicide is six times higher than females.
* Among the elderly (sixty-five through eighty-five and on, 84 percent of the suicides are male).

More disturbing is the fact that men born in the late 1950s and early 1960s are 50 percent more likely to commit suicide than their fathers' generation. Young men, who are now between twenty-five and twenty-nine, are twice as likely to kill themselves as their grandfathers.

Why is this happening? Men's power to win and even to survive is lost. Driven to despair, a man surrenders. Allow me to give you analogy. With adequate ammunition, arms, and military support, the warrior fights on. He has the power to win, and at the very least, to survive. With ammunition depleted and military support weak, the soldier begins to lose hope.

This is very apropos of today's dilemma. The problem with many men today is that they do not know where the enemies are coming from that are attacking their inner strength and psychological well-being. They are not aware of who is firing the silent bullets that are hitting them. The high levels of stress men are facing today and the lack of social and individual support are some of the forceful adversaries impacting men's abilities to direct their lives. Men feel lost and socially isolated. They are not in touch with the sources that nurture their strength.

Feeling a lack of power, they often give up—if not to final self-destruction, they surrender to other destructive devices, such as drugs, alcohol, excessive eating, or dangerous escapades, while they should be seeking higher purposes. These self-defeating ways of coping with the attacks on their self-worth affect men's longevity and health. When a man loses his core purpose and what is essential to him, he is lost.

When facing times like these, it would be advisable to ask for direction and help, even though it is not a man's natural inclination to do so. Admitting weakness takes an act of strength and intelligence. I'm going to repeat that: admitting weakness takes an act of strength and intelligence because the defect can be corrected and a purpose laid out that perhaps wasn't there before.

Longevity and Health

In America, the life span of a man is seven years less than that of a woman. Yet in 1920, women in the United States lived only one year longer than men. Today, women's longevity has increased seven times over that of men's. Would you be shocked to know that it's not solely the women's nagging that is causing this? American men have twice as many deaths from liver disease and three times the deaths from heart attacks than women.

Studies show how so many of these early deaths can be prevented with simple alterations of habits and excessive lifestyles, as mentioned above. One of my main objectives is to relay the concept of what the 21st century man, who currently feels immortal, can do in his twenties and thirties to prevent long-range ill effects in his fifties, sixties, and beyond.

Men are twice as likely to die from cancer than women. It saddens me to no end that men suffer from this condition that, in some cases, is preventable. One main cause is that men are too embarrassed to get checked out and screened. Imagine that! Adopting a healthier lifestyle and seeing your doctor more frequently, even complaining of some symptoms, could very well save your life. It is my hope that the 21st twenty-first-century young man gets a grip on this before it gets a grip on him.

Men take more dangerous and life-threatening jobs than women. Ninety-seven percent of job-related injuries and deaths are male. In school, 80 percent to 90 percent of children with behavioral and learning problems are boys. Men are three times more likely to be murdered and victims of violence than women.

Regarding divorce, though about 50 percent of marriages fail, women start breakups by a two-to-three margin. This indicates that more women push men out than vice versa. By a far wider margin, women get the children, the monthly checks, and the houses, even though they may have separate incomes. Of the homeless population, 85 percent are men.

The point of all of these examples is to wake you up about some of the issues and grave problems that the male gender is having today. Remember, knowledge is power. Being aware is the first step in coming to grips with the challenges men are facing. *Prevent the preventable!*

Women Are Outperforming Men

Gentlemen, are you ready for these statistics?

* Women make up nearly 58% percent of today's college graduates.
* In community and four-year colleges, only about 45 percent of the undergraduates are men.
* Women graduate from law school at about the same rate as men, and they make up nearly half of medical-school graduates.
* More women than men are earning advanced degrees.
* Nine percent of women and 6 percent of men hold either a master's or professional degree.
* There are now more women in the workforce than men.
* In 150 of the biggest cities in the United States, the median full-time salaries of young women are 8 percent higher than those of the guys in their peer group. In two cities, Atlanta and Memphis, those women are making about 20 percent more. In various other cities, it ranged from 12 percent to 17 percent.

Though the earnings of women in law, medical, and other careers are somewhat less than men's earnings, this is changing. Regarding wealth, the US Census Bureau reports that women who are heads of households have a net worth over 140 percent greater than men who are heads of households.

Women have more voting power than men. In 2004, 60 percent of women voted, and just 56 percent of men voted. In a close race, the nearly nine million more votes that women carry is enough to swing an election in their favor.

These numbers do not paint the male species as winners. At the very least, they affirm that women today are doing better than men in financial, educational, and career markets. Their health is significantly better. Women have arrived. Men have to work harder and smarter if they don't want to be second-class citizens compared to women.

The 21st century man has to literally shape up to keep his health in order, and he must empower himself to do better in education, career, and lifestyles, over which women have gained advantages. Otherwise, he can always find himself a sugar mama.

The Patriarchy Is Dead

Men's personal superiority a century ago, once called the patriarchy, is gone. Yet many women still blame their problems on this outdated concept. Today, women can pursue any careers they want, any businesses or properties they desire, any colleges they choose, and they can gain positions of high political power.

Moreover, the governmental policies, laws, and colleges with curricula in women's studies support women, but there is not much support for men. How many men's studies classes do you encounter in the universities?

Another Kick to the Balls: The Media

Where are the days of the *Dragnet* and *Perry Mason* shows? They depicted men as powerful, responsible, and intelligent.

Men were men. Today's television, perhaps to a lesser degree than films, misrepresent men as boyish, inept, socially clumsy, and bumbling skirt chasers and bad boys. Also, compared to women, they are usually lacking in one way or another.

The reason is that the frequency of men's incapacities, compared to women in the media, is not uncommon. In most households, women hold the purchasing power, and networks are focused on that demographic. And for that reason, women are held in a higher regard.

Research has shown that not only were men portrayed negatively on television, but they were also portrayed as metrosexual and were feminized. The moral of the story (pun intended) is to take television and film with a grain of salt. Do not allow it to be your training ground and catalyst for manhood.

Enough with Male Bashing

The negative messages that men are goofballs and are lacking are finally being recognized by men and various high-end brands across the board in the media. These men-at-fault messages, which have become ingrained within the collective mentality of pop culture, aren't as accepted and popular. Where they once portrayed debasing competence, worth, and disrespect for men, the times are changing. Men are finally being portrayed as fathers, husbands, and good guys, as it should be. Male bashing is not acceptable; it is a form of rejection that promotes some predictable reactions. As a 21st century young man, you will not heed these negative images portrayed by the media and will focus on what empowers and supports your self-esteem.

Media Outlets for Men

The good news about the digital age is that the majority of media outlets are truly supportive of men; this includes life and style columns as well as issues. I believe that seeking positive news is always advantageous in becoming a better man and honing your skills to being a superior man.

A few great digital forums are Askmen.com, *Forbes, USA Today, GQ, Men's Fitness*, and, of course, my favorite, the *Wall Street Journal*. As stated above, don't allow yourself to get sucked into the digital era, especially into outlets that degrade men. This especially includes social media. With so many choices today, seek out the best to be the best.

Overcompensation

Feelings of inferiority will normally cause depression, yet they also lend their hands to overcompensation, such as testing reasonable limits. Overdoing what seem manly covers up the feelings of inferiority that male bashing (lack of respect, reduced status, and undervaluing a man's worth) gives rise to. Types of overcompensating are compulsive overworking, extreme physical activity, exposure to danger, delinquent and criminal deeds, and striving beyond one's limits.

Fierce and intimidating-looking tattoos, sloppy dress, long and unkempt beards, fast and powerful cars, and blunt and vulgar language also provide illusions of manly strength and importance. These are all physical symbols of manliness, yet they do not define the inborn, deep, masculine strength.

Though one-sided devotion to sports, money making, and careers bring approval, some power, and what the common culture marks as a "successful man," the price is high. This effort to reach the high spot often bankrupts the interior truth of the man and frequently degrades his physical and mental health as the years progress.

The 21st century man is prudent. He watches carefully not to exceed his limits so that it will not damage his health emotionally and mentally. He will not do it for short gains. You're a long-range planner and will not impair your health for the illusion of strength.

Battling the Bashing: The Way of the 21st Century Man

The direct and indirect insults to his self-worth should drive a man to reinstate his power and dignity. He does not have to apologize or take bashing from any source, whether from individuals, institutions, laws, politics, media, or negative attitudes.

The 21st century man strives to become aware of the realities that box him in and are hostile to his healthy growth. He uses his intelligence and senses like a radar to avoid avenues of belief, work, and people that lead him to dead ends. He does this by developing qualities of his entire brain and nurturing his physical, emotional, social, artistic, and spiritual growth. By exerting consistent effort to becoming balanced, whole, and in harmony with his unspoken inner voice, he then becomes an empowered man unto himself. He stands on two legs.

Failure to take this action puts the contemporary male at the mercy of the disordered and historical changes evolving now in this century. Unaware that the guidelines of manhood are unclear, he flops around, seeking the better and hoping the worse does not happen. Being aware and working toward the goal of complete manhood vastly increases the odds for success in just about every aspect of his life.

Purpose fosters knowledge, especially in today's world, and that is power. It takes courage to pursue a goal that is not yet recognized, much less approved, by the collective mind-set. It takes warrior level of strength to challenge the outdated values of the nineteenth and twentieth centuries that are still in circulation. And it takes smart thinking to sort out goals and values that are helpful and worth keeping from those that are obsolete. The 21st century man looks ahead.

Using time effectively for activities that pay off is an absolute requirement, for the price of success is to give up the popular distractions and escapes, especially to the clever hooks of visual media, which contrives to capture the vital time and attention of the unmindful.

THE EVOLVING 21ST CENTURY

This is a time of the unraveling of the past. The beliefs of the economic, political, and social systems of the nineteenth and twentieth centuries are being tested. Do they work or not? Are they effective now? Which ones should be kept or modified? What opportunities are arising out of the era that is emerging?

Global communication, the efficiency of manufacturing, overpopulation, urbanization, heating up the planet, computers and automation, robots, the proliferation of atomic threats, long-range missiles, the interweaving of religious and social systems, and the rapidity of all this change have consequences. These changes affect everyone on the planet, either directly or indirectly, for better or worse. The 21st century is in its adolescence and not yet fully formed or understood. Therefore, the task for young men of this period in history is to scout for the signs of change be aware and ready to navigate successfully through 21st Century and where it's heading—and, perhaps, to even lead the way to a better century.

Scattered Thinking

It is the norm for a growing adolescent to be confused and experimental. After trying this and that for a while, the young person picks a direction and sets out on a path. Conflicts gradually resolve themselves, and scattered energy unifies to win a goal. Likewise, as it is in the early stages of development, the 21st century is following a similar trend.

Fragmented thought bites and undigested information define the mixed, collective mind of today. Chunks of philosophy and religious beliefs, mingled gender roles, varied and niche groups, and alternative lifestyles have not yet been sorted out.

Choices and ideas abound everywhere, but few know in which direction to go or the sure way. These new ideas are in the process of being set in place. Nevertheless, the alternate, ineffective, blurred, and weakly defined courses of action continue to volley back and forth and threaten the uniformed. This is the time to understand what a valuable hierarchy of values is and what is worth living for. As we are smack-dab in the midst of the information era, it is imperative to be guided by a wise elder, either currently living or in the past. Evolving in your way of thinking and choices will make you, the 21st century man more judicious, and you will gain clarity amid the plethora of scatter and confusion.

Going Backward

Those who are unable to cope with uncertainty and the rapidly changing spirit of the times have problems. Additionally, these people are often the problems themselves. They seek security and the "true way" by going backward to an obsolete past, which is almost always painted romantically. They falsely believe that the views of past ages were superior to the present, and they envision a utopia, such as an imagined community or society that possesses highly desirable or nearly perfect qualities for its citizens. They embrace out-of-date and inflexible beliefs and fight the changes that advanced knowledge brings forward.

Their beliefs often do not permit a "live and let live" attitude. Many men and their perspectives toward manhood fall into this backward viewpoint. As a result, conflict and tension are created because knowledge that is moving forward always opposes the tug backward. As an enlightened and strong 21st century man, you will challenge the efficacy of these beliefs— before they challenge you. The times are changing with or without you. Being proactive, educated, and awake allows the modern man to help make the change a successful one. Take the reins, and help guide the future to a successful destination.

Shifts in the 21st Century

Rapidly shifting economies and technologies, an overpopulated planet, global and rapid communication, and earth changes are hardly recent news. But the sum of their impacts is rarely discussed. Moreover, the consequences of their combined impact on the lives of young men struggling to make their ways in a paradigm shift is often ignored. Do you understand the significance of this paragraph?

These facts, though denied in some cases, can have radical repercussions, and the accumulated force of the changes is powerful enough to demand sober thinking. This is straight-up man talk—no beating around the bushes here.

The 21st century man has to think out of the box and wrap his head around the impact of the current shifts taking place. Hopefully, he will be proactive in setting the course for a better century.

Skilled, Motivated, and Low-Wage Billions

It is common knowledge that business goes where the labor is cheap. Those places are in Asia and in other developing countries. The workers are technically skilled and motivated to learn. They perform favorably and at the same level as workers in developed countries, yet for far cheaper wages. Higher-paid wage earners in America and Europe put business at a disadvantage in markets that compete globally. As a result, economic pressure will continue to push business abroad and choke wages in developed countries.

The 21st century is bringing much more competition, and it is getting much harder for the modern man to get a good-paying job. The competition is stiff, to be sure.

What can be done? Get creative, competitive, and educated. The competition is certainly keen but lacking in "out-of-the-box thinking." Other countries aren't as adept in this arena. Be the innovator!

Computers and "Thinking" Robots

Automation and increasingly sophisticated software allow any job that has a pattern or ordered system to be sent to foreign suppliers of low-wage, skilled workers.

The efficiency of automation dramatically reduces the need for human beings, as illustrated with the introduction of ATMs, when five hundred thousand teller positions quickly evaporated within a few years.

Practically everyone knows someone kicked into unemployment or reduced wages due to smart machines. Robots are in line to reduce labor needs in food- and hotel-service areas, once considered immune from the software pruning shears. Some analysts predict that 30 percent of ordinary jobs will be replaced by smart robots by 2025. These robots with advanced software will replace much of the low-wage work that is sent overseas and will replace related jobs in North America—not to mention that the jobs that are left will have drastically reduced wages.

This vital information isn't to scare the reader; it is to make you smarter and more aware of what is going on. Again, be creative, innovative, and educated. Stay abreast of the times.

The Internet

The Internet has knitted the world together, and it continues to bring a powerful change, as significant as the printed word did in the fifteenth century. However, the jury is still out on how the Internet affects people overall. While it has increased information, it has also created a tremendous amount of chaos and confusion in the information age.

The modern young man will need to decipher the depth of information because we're not sure whether it's true or false. Just because it's on the net doesn't mean that it is fact. The depth of truth is brought by experience. Caution should be heeded in discerning what is published as fact or fiction.

On the bright side of things, it has brought numerous opportunities, markets, and information to the forefront that were previously not easily available. It is a high-octane fuel for the 21st century, and it is unlike any other in history.

Overpopulation and Megacities

According to the United Nations, the world will try to house nine billion people by 2040. Some predictions put the population as high as eleven billion by 2050. For every billion more, life gets harder for everyone and probably much worse for the ongoing extinction of plants and animals (except for bacteria).

Though most of the population increase is happening in developing regions, most rural inhabitants will swarm to the cities. Already, half of the world's population lives in urban areas. By 2050, about 84 percent of the citizens in the developed countries will live (perhaps a better word is *survive*) within the urban sprawl.

This shift from country to city is a phenomenon of the 21st century. It is an unprecedented historical change in humankind's culture—not only in social roots, which have been the foundation from the beginning of civilization, but also in the grounded and secured identities of traditional families, communities, nations, tribes, and religious communities. The effects of these shifts tend to fractionate and pull people apart, undermining their senses of security, both personally and in families.

There are advantages to be gained from urban living for some who have connections and capital. But the crowding, congestion, pollution, and infrastructure stress from the large influx of people also bring to the surface more regulations, laws, and complexity. On the whole, the effect produces more obstacles to hack through in order to establish a good living.

As these shifts occur, the young men of the 21st century will have more roadblocks and congestion to deal with, which will make life more complex, harder, and time-consuming. Planning ahead and being more flexible will help navigate through the morass of this congestion. Save, save, and invest as much money as possible, because the expenses in the big cities will increase. Be as conservative as possible in spending.

More Working Years

The number of people in the workforce who are aging is increasing in developed countries. Some economists speculate that this condition may create jobs for the young in health services. However, people are living and working longer with better health. Others in solid financial states and good health are opting to work until they drop. On the downside, many cannot afford to retire and need to keep working.

Companies are starting to provide for older workers and are using special technology to aid their productivity. The saying that seventy is the new sixty and forty is the new thirty are realities. Even the retirement age has increased—hence, the conversation we're having.

This theme is found again: fewer job openings for more job seekers. And who knows when retirement will be for the 21st century man? With all the advice given thus far, it's pretty easy to discern where we're going with this. Begin to invest earlier for your future and retirement—even five or ten dollars to begin with, as you grow in your field of work. You'll be amazed at how fast it accumulates.

Capitalism, Abundance, and Meaning

One of the greatest efficiencies and major strengths in the business model of capitalism is that it produces an abundance and unlimited variety of goods. Along with the products comes an army of marketers to sell them. Unfortunately, the problem is that there are more products than buyers, so selling them becomes a premium job. Without ads and clever marketers to seduce consumers to buy what they do not need, the economy would collapse.

When people's bellies, homes, and garages are full, they tend to bend to the social impact of "impressing," with or without meaning. Because they have more than enough, their interests alter from just needing something to use to wanting something that tells who they are and how they wish to be perceived or valued. The meaning then becomes about external beauty and a problematic sense of self-worth.

This is the next stage that motivates people to buy. The forward-looking 21st century young man will do more than merely engineering utilitarian products. To have the advantage, he will emphasize his right brain functions—artistic, intuitive, and feeling sensitivities—to form a view of the whole picture and take note of people's untapped desires. The best examples are the Apple iPhone and iPad. They are aesthetically pleasing and functional, and they serve purposes.

Supply and demand will always be around, especially in today's society. Be the 21st century man who makes a significant difference in what the public needs and desires. If you're a leader who wishes to be a business owner, focus on ever-changing trends, and follow those whom you admire, such as Steve Jobs, Elon Musk, or Mark Cuban.

If you're not vying to be a business owner, then ever-growing positions such as doctors, lawyers, engineers, builders, marketers, and even male nurses make great money. Become the best man you can by providing excellence in whatever field you choose.

The Years 2020 and 2024: More Uncertain Changes

As an educational psychologist, I've come across many personalities in my career. One evening, as I was hanging out with my Mensa friends, I met a gentleman named Jack. He introduced me to astrology, and my fascination began. I've found that it provides valuable information on events, people, and places. Astrology has over five thousand years of validation. As I am a highly educated and intellectual man, it would seem to be at odds with my persona. However, I've found much validation in astrology, and as a man of the 21st century; I believe it to be very valuable for you as well. Sir Issac Newton, when questioned about the validity of astrology, said, "I've studied the matter, you sir, have not." No less a brilliant man of the ages, Albert Einstein stated, "Astrology is a science in itself and contains an illuminating body of knowledge. It taught me many things and I am greatly indebted to it." If those two geniuses believed, perhaps it's not a far reach for you. Let's have some fun nonetheless.

Jupiter and Saturn will join together in the same sign of Aquarius in December of 2020. Some astrologers say that this conjunction is significant because, for the first time in 180 years, the Jupiter-Saturn conjunct will leave the earth signs, Capricorn, Taurus, and Virgo. This means a major shift in philosophy and ideology. It will be very group-oriented—a rise in brotherhood, if you will. For instance, there will be a rise in unions and so forth. It will be a time of coming together with ideas, intelligence, and even more advanced technological innovations. A shift of deeper, unconventional thinking will alter the dumbing-down of America.

Then, four years later, Pluto will move into Aquarius. This will reinforce what we stated above and will also bring more technological and political changes. They will be extremely powerful. Evidence of this was found between 1777 and 1799, the last time Pluto was in Aquarius. A paradigm shift of the Western world occurred: the American Revolutionary War, the Constitution, the Bill of Rights, and the French Revolution. These were big, political changes that favored the common man at the expense of tyrants and kings. This move in these major planets from earthbound energies to air-thinking energies should signal a shift from money making and getting things as the top values to questioning and realigning previous attitudes and beliefs.

Emphasis on self-expression, concern for the common good of the group, and even more technological advances should arise. The economic and political-power elites, especially the backward, conservative ones, should face considerable opposition from innovative ideas. Political and economic priorities are likely to alter radically. The changes could happen quite quickly. It will not be business as usual, and the changes could turn many systems and structures upside down.

21st Century America: The Loss of the American Dream(er)

Most recently, I read an article on www.washingtonsblog.com that only confirms how hard becoming a successful American man in the 21st century may be. The article is entitled "Rags to Riches: Much Easier in Scandinavia than America" with a leading sentence of "The American dream is now spoken with a Scandinavian accent." The Organisation for Economic Co-operation and Development (OECD) finds that social mobility between generations is dramatically lower in the United States than in many other developed countries. The report finds that the United States ranks well below Denmark,

Australia, Norway, Finland, Canada, Sweden, Germany, and Spain in terms of how freely citizens move up or down the social ladder. Only in Italy and Great Britain is the intensity of the relationship between individual and parental earnings even greater. America was ranked number 10. Though these statistics are hard to swallow, as a young man of the 21st century, you know that working harder and smarter and creating a competitive edge for yourself will benefit you.

Class Society: Few on the Top

Warren Buffet said "There's class warfare, all right, but it's my class, the rich class, that's making war, and we're winning." Here is a class society: about 1 percent of the US population owns about 40 percent of the nation's wealth. The top 20 percent owns about 80 percent of it. America is very much a class society, with a few doing well. The rest, including what is left of the middle class, are being paid barely adequate wages. Others are lucky to have jobs and luckier if the businesses they work for allow them to keep jobs for a reasonable time. Then, consider the obscene pay of CEOs, who have the highest pay ratio in the world compared to the pay of the workers under them. Historically, the gap between the "haves and have not" is too big; it sets up the conditions for significant political and social change. We are now beginning to experience the social and economic divide.

So the 21st century man cannot sit by the wayside and watch. If you don't wish to be pressured by the system, then become politically aware, and participate. Those who don't do haven't any room to complain.

Control and the Cost of an Education

Violence and debt are the two most efficient and effective ways the powers use to control people. Most students have accumulated significant debt. Some have enough debt that it nearly equals the cost of a house. Some school loans made with private lenders do not permit students to dissolve the debt, even when they have declared bankruptcy. Yet the loaner can go bankrupt and be bailed out by the government. This has happened recently. This student-loan issue is serious because most students have significant debt after completing their studies.

The young man graduates and then becomes an indentured servant to the bank for decades, even if he has a decent-paying job. Consider that the interest on the loan accrues each month, adding to the debt burden, since starting a new job, which is generally low paying, does not permit a timely payoff of the debt.

The need for highly skilled jobs that require many years of study, coupled with the high cost of tuition, blows apart the old commandment "Work hard, and you will succeed." In fact, you may work hard and long and build up debt, or work hard at two or three jobs, just to make ends meet. The point is that the high cost of getting an education, coupled with insufficient pay, does not service the debt or allow for independent living. This challenges the mythos of America as the land of opportunity and the American dream(er).

It is the land of opportunity only for the few that can afford it. According to some professional economists, most folks in the United States can look forward to low-paying jobs, low-cost housing, and in general, low-cost living. Those with heavy loads of student debt will need to delay planning for marriage and family, a decent house to live in, and the ability to dig out of the economic ghettos into which they have fallen.

Here are two questions to think about: Will you gain value from a high-cost education? This brings up the question: What is the purpose of an education? Researching statistics will benefit the 21st century young man greatly in determining the worth of getting a degree and what major he will choose.

THE FULL IMPACT: IT IS GETTING HARDER

A dding up the trends—explosive population growth, abundant foreign labor, job-cutting automation, climate change, thirst for fresh water, pollution, congested megacities, expensive education, proliferation of atomic weapons, and gaps between the haves and have-nots, as well as the uncertainty of the future—it is easy to see that life has become harder. And now we're dealing with situations that are more expensive, time-consuming, complex, irritating, and unstable, making us anxious.

No matter where you look at the emerging 21st century, whether left, right, up, or down, living has become more difficult, complicated, and overcrowded in nearly every category. It also has more delays because of congestion and fewer degrees of freedom, with limited escape doors. Yet with all of this complexity and the technology boom, new opportunities arise.

Changes Offer New Opportunities

The unraveling of past economic, social, and global orders opens up avenues of possibilities. As the population ages and more people retire, the doors that have long been closed are opening. The rapid change has created a complexity of systems and well-populated niche markets, which are global, as well as technological innovations that beg for advanced skills and specialized knowledge.

The 21st century young man uses both sides of his brain. Besides educating himself on the upward trends of technical knowledge, he will also focus on human studies, especially the different needs and viewpoints of various cultures and personalities of people and their aesthetic sensitivities. He will broaden his fundamental skills by including out-of-the-box-thinking within the social and economic awareness needed to tap new markets, both domestic and abroad.

Learning foreign languages and undertaking wide-range travel can teach these skills even more realistically than books or computers. The rapid pace of innovation, technology, and global marketing has put a premium on learning and being flexible, thereby adapting to many innovations in jobs in the marketplace.

This is important for the young man of today because many jobs are in line to be outdated, downsized due to automation, or sent out of the country. Staying stuck in one line of work or in one skill set is not the position of the awake and ready man of this century.

Cashing In on the Opportunities

The 21st century man who does not want to be ground down should not stay in one place. Mediocre jobs with barely livable pay are available around the corner in your local neighborhood. Cashing in on the new opportunities presented today demands out-of-the-box thinking (I'm going to pound that home) and courage to make U-turns in directions that are opposite from where everyone else is going. It requires an open, adventurous mind-set to travel where the opportunities arise. Fear has no place!

Better jobs with career potential require going to different places in both mind and location. You're a conceptual thinker, especially in data analysis, where fishing out the relevant information from the factoids is useful for any job category. The 21st century man sets up a pattern of lifelong learning and plans ahead for living to ninety and beyond. He digs deeply within to know about himself, learns about others foreign to him, and strives to be a complete and mature man. Such goals will not interfere with a path to success in work or in happiness, but being stuck and single-minded will.

Learning to Learn

A college education is not necessarily the ticket to job and career success. The high expense to earn a worthwhile college degree with a problematic payoff puts its value at risk. Only about half of the jobs require a college diploma. We covered this.

The Man You Can Be For The 21st Century

So let's dig a bit deeper. After all, it is your future. All jobs require the ability to read, write, add, and think. Almost every category of construction, manufacturing, technology, and services are open avenues for ambitious young men. However, due to enormous competition and rapid change, the approach to learning and the ability to keep the better jobs requires a mental-software update.

The ability to follow directions intelligently and social skills in dealing with employers and coworkers are necessary for doing well on any job. However, the more desirable jobs favor creative, artistic, and social awareness. This suggests using both sides of the brain, developing all parts of the personality, and striving to be a complete man. Unfortunately, it still rings true, even today, that a man is a machine to be used, though subtly covered up with more highly processed hypocrisy.

However, you, the 21st century man, works on being a success within your essential manliness while striving to be competent, if not excellent, in your chosen work, whether you're a CEO or a garbage collector. The old approach to manhood ignored a consideration of the well-being of the inner man. It simply did not matter to the business's employers or military to take into account the quality of the man's life, provided that he did his work.

You may face that today, but you know your worth both internally and externally. As you move up in your position and even strive to be the boss, you can change this dynamic. Until then, you are secure in who you are and what you're capable of.

Measure of the 21st Century Man

The 21st century man is unconventional. The new manhood is measured not only by what he has attained in the material or financial worlds but his worth is also measured by his internal standards. This man tunes into his inner truth in harmony with the quality of his work, achievement, honing skills, and social and civic responsibilities.

There is an adage that I truly believe in: Know thyself. In today's society, this is quite the irony and is in contradiction to what most men believe and/or were taught. Cultivating the truths of your inner self as well as artful living—being cordial, understanding the importance of being pleasant, having values and goals that are worth living for, and taking care of yourself with concern for others—will help you immensely to gain material success, especially in the long run.

Knowing about yourself, making consistent effort to live to your high purpose, and planning for the long run greatly reduces the odds of making a mess of your life sometime down the road, which many unreflective men often do.

The Man for the 21st Century: Whole, Connected, Strong

It's just a fact that some men envy other men who are more successful or stronger, are put together better, have the hot girlfriend/wife, and have more toys, which then begs the questions that many men ask themselves: "Do I measure up?"; "How do I get that?"; "Do I have the stuff to navigate throughout the blitz of obstacles that are going to be thrown at me to get there?"; "Am I smart and strong enough?"

The answers do not come from following a list of ingredients for man-making. Unfortunately, ideas and thinking about taking action and doing something productive stay in the head and go around in circles. The head-tripping male gets stuck and does not move effectively, often not realizing that his goals are won by taking action, not through hoping, wishing, and sitting in his comfort zone.

Becoming a man is a process of searching, experimenting, failing, and finding your place in the scheme of things and learning to accept your limits. It is important to kiss your failures because they are great teachers. Undertaking the aim of full manhood is a continuing effort to fuse one's abilities, skills, and dreams into success in the material world while being in harmony with the truth of one's inner world.

In psychological terms, it means, in a general sense, balancing the extroverted personality that is action and concerned with outer things with the introverted personality that is concerned with feelings and intuition. It is a lifelong work that endures into a man's nineties and even longer. A man's strength increases as his outer actions become unified with his inner being.

The 21st century man is hopeful, optimistic, and far-reaching because he is able to look at the present and intelligently pick, choose, and cultivate things that will help his future. He is fully aware and cautious of negative powers and energies that control and undermine his rightful status and worth. He is sensitive to what saps and depletes his energy and to those who suck it dry and drag him down. Conversely, the 21st century man stands on two legs and takes off with two wings. He is informed about a broader and more advanced view of manhood.

Old Ideals of Manhood

For the most part, the old ideals of manhood spell out a narrow, one-sided, and limited model of what a man should be. Primitive, tribal, underdeveloped, and postmodern societies looked upon men as a meal ticket, protector, and baby maker.

The Man You Can Be For The 21ˢᵗ Century

In primitive and tribal societies, the man had to hunt and bring in the meat, fish, and herd and, in some cases, steal the cattle—dangers, wounds, and pain be damned. If he did not kill, everyone in the tribe went hungry.

The man brought in provisions to feed the family. He took on the warrior's fight to defend his territory and claim more of it by spear, arrow, sword, or gun. Thereby, he preserved the food supply.

The guidelines were clear and rigid. Defending against wild animals, greedy neighbors, and fickle weather meant the difference between starving, eating, or getting a spear in the stomach. It makes sense that the strong, courageous, alert, risk-taking men should be esteemed. The group's survival depended on those qualities and still does in many parts of the world. Men raised their boys to be these great, courageous, and tough men.

Though hunting is more for sport, men are still expected to churn out widgets, bring in money, and feed their families. Unfortunately, in this day and age, there are manipulative business practices that steal by invisible deceits through lawyers, hackers, and shady businessmen. A man's worth was and still is today measured to a large degree by his ability to provide for his family and his "tribe," to protect them, and to expand them by procreating.

It Can Be Summed Up by the Three P's: Provide, Protect, Procreate

In the past, the three P's for a man were are all external, extroverted actions that didn't take into account any of his inner life, desires, and dreams. The choices were very limited for many reasons, and how true a man could be to his internal truth was dismissed. The archetypal pattern still exists today, but it is different because a man today can follow his dreams and be true to himself, in addition to the three P's. Growth to full and whole manhood is easier today. This is the main difference between the past and present ideals of manhood.

Today, food and goods are abundant, so physical survival is reasonably secure. The standard of living continues to rise because necessities are taken for granted. Leisure time, education, and alternatives in numerous avenues of living are available. Growth to full manhood, emotional and spiritual well-being, and self-reliance are now open to men in this modern age.

Times have changed so drastically that men are no longer the only gender needed to protect and to provide for the tribe. Nor do they need to be a fifty-hour-a-week, money-churning ATM. In this modern day and age, men have a plethora of choices, much like women do.

The economic, social, and global changes forming the 21st century encourage the choices that expand and unify a male's capacity to be a full man. Unlike their ancestors who didn't have the options to develop their inner masculinity and strength, today's men do (and should) take full advantage of these opportunities. As we said in the previous chapter, honing into a man's deep purpose will catalyze his masculine energy, which allows him to overcome obstacles and endure to the very end, thereby fulfilling his essential and vital purpose.

Men today have the opportunity to develop broader, deeper, fuller, and more satisfying identities.

THE THREE STANDARD TYPES OF MALES AND THE 21ST CENTURY, 4TH DIMENSIONAL MAN

The Glorified Male

As we've discussed in the previous chapter, in the primitive and tribal societies, it was the man who hunted, the warrior who defended against enemies, and the farmer who brought in the harvest and multiplied the cows. This is what the cultures have and continue to set up as the ideal. In contemporary, materialistic society, it is the male who makes it to the top of the food chain, whereby the standard of his success is measured by money. The glory goes to the multimillionaire, the celebrity, the sport champion, and the successful businessman.

Today's culture discounts the means by which he worked to gain his profits and fame. How he made his money is far less important than the number of zeros he has in the bank. What society does care about or considers is how much he's worth. That is the glorified male's worth.

Not much else counts, even if he is a war hero or adds to the well-being of his community. Without the zeros, he is just another nice guy who gets a pat on the back. Though his local community will acknowledge him—even consider him prestigious to a degree—society will not reward him with power or riches.

The Alternative Male

In contrast to the glorified male, the alternative male (including artists of all varieties, actors, clergymen, spiritual seekers, nerds, those with same-sex orientation, research scientists, intellectuals, and writers) does not measure his well-being by things or his bank account. Buying and spending are not the means to his happiness. Consumerism is not his religion.

Though accepted and respected in their fields, these men can do very well financially and can benefit society, yet they are not considered "fully equipped" as men. They may be perceived as having weaknesses that distracts from the conventional views and standards of glorified masculinity.

On the other hand, for the alternative man, his passion, his dreams, and his being true to himself define his identity and fortify his well-being. Some are extremely fortunate to have made a lot of money and earned fame, yet they kept their inner truths intact and were not swayed by public demand, nor did they sell their souls to the marketplace. Notable examples are Prince, Russell Brand, Tony Robbins, and Blake Mycoskie, owner of TOMS Shoes.

Many men who are not lucky enough to be gifted with these extraordinary talents may take other courses. They link their passions with compatible means to make good money.

Here is an excellent example: John is a distant relative of mine in his forties. He is happily married and is a fine father of two beautiful children. From childhood, he always wanted to be a musician. But it did not provide him sufficient income to raise a family. So he integrated music with his two other interests, mathematics and computer science. He has a company that develops software for the music industry, thereby allowing him to stay within the realm of his passion, and he continues to play his music while supporting his family.

Allow me to use myself as an example, too. I love oil painting, traveling, and fly-fishing. Neither of these dream passions provides the standard of living that I desire. I knew early on in my teens that I would become a psychologist, and to this day, I am very proud of my choices. To keep a balance on my work and passions, I carefully managed my time and work schedule. I was able to paint ten to twelve hours a week and take about four weeks a year to fly-fish. My job provided me with an income so I could travel. There was a price in my desires to fulfill my passions—I made less money. The lasting and deep satisfaction I receive from fulfilling my heart's desires still make me laugh at the absent dollars.

The alternative male marches to a different drummer. He values and seeks his inner truth first rather than competing for top place or hauling in truckloads of money. This kind of man protects his life force and individuality over material rewards.

Men of the Opposition

There are two types of "men of the opposition." The first includes those who break the rules illegally. Criminals, gangsters, organized crime members, cyber thieves, and corporate embezzlers represent the domestic variety of illegal offenders. These types disrupt the well-being of society for their own selfish profit. They have no concern for the society they exploit or the victims they harm.

Violent revolutionaries and terrorists are less personally selfish, though more violent, than the criminal group. They cause injury for idealistic reasons. They aim at undoing the powerful elite and the order of government. They are very dangerous because they can create mass chaos and sometimes do.

The second type of "men of the opposition" take legal action to change governmental, corporate, economic, social, and environmental policies. Fortunately, political parties, environmental advocates, nonprofit organizations, charities, and many other action groups seek to correct what they view as unfair and ineffective policies. Lawsuits, publications, education, and economic support are some of the means they use to reform the existing state of affairs.

Both groups challenge and contradict the "norms" of society and have senses of defiance. The first group gains power and money and may lose their lives and freedom with long stints in prison. The second group goes about their opposition legally and works diligently to correct errors in the system. They believe in their causes and often find ways to get their messages across, if not altogether make changes that are significant. I look forward to the 21st century young men overwhelmingly choosing the latter.

THE ADVANCED, 21ST CENTURY MAN OF 4 DIMENSIONS

The evolving man of this new century puts together the strengths of the glorified, alternative, and oppositional males. He defines a new category and concept of manhood and masculinity. The 21st century 4th dimensional young man is broader, stronger, more organized, more flexible, more adaptable, far more integrated, and smarter than the traditional-man ideal. He takes on the goal of achieving and earning enough money to live well according to his own terms while honoring his inner self and standing firm to his "own" resolve in becoming a 21st century man—in opposition to the old norms of masculinity.

21st Century Glorified Male
To be the 21st century "glorified male" is to be one who has the work skills, makes a sufficient amount of money, and has expendable income. He cannot live paycheck to paycheck. He

will strive for the proper education and diligent work skills that will allow him to live in commodious surroundings, supersede the cost-of-living expenses, and explore opportunities and travel, which will allow him to expand his horizons in every regard—mentally, physically, spiritually, emotionally, and economically. His hard-core desire for material success will not supersede his internal values and life.

However, without the due diligence stated above, he will deplete the reservoir of his male energy to work night and day to service his debts to the banks. His opportunities for sexual play will suffer from the stress of overwork, worry, and insecurity. And what male wants that?

21st Century Alternative Male

The evolving man of the 21st century takes on the attitude of the alternative male by honoring his unique self. He studies and cultivates his nature and traits that distinguish him from others. By knowing his individuality, he is able to tap into the energy fueled by the desires unique to him.

The extra charge of energy he captures by being his true self helps him overcome the obstacles that stand in the way of his successful achievement of excellence in his work.

21st Century Man of the Opposition

The 21st century man must have tremendous courage and discipline to be a man of the opposition. He carries a vision that is broader, richer, and more far-reaching than ideals of manhood that are stuck in time zones long past.

He is cognizant and strives to learn about the many facets of life, has a clear vision and plans his life intelligently, thereby setting himself apart from the cultural norm. He is a man who keeps track of where he is going and has a pretty good idea of how to get there. He then becomes a superior competitor of those who are still running out-of-date mind tapes of what males should have been in the nineteenth and twentieth centuries.

The oppositional young man of the future takes risks. His self-understanding and capacity to think for himself makes him less vulnerable to the clever scams that try to pick his pocket and to the touted paths that lead him nowhere.

So he then becomes a threat to the political and economic manipulators. Nothing upsets the powers more than people who smell the crap a mile away and know where it is coming from.

The whole is greater than the sum of its parts.

Now, you have the three powerful components of masculinity to make yourself a 4th Dimensional Man who is growing and striving to be whole, complete, and strong. Like the Empire State Building, the whole is greater than the millions of materials that it's made of. The sum is greater than its parts.

THE RIGHT STATE OF MIND

When To #JustSayNo

The various ways a young man on his way to adult manhood disconnects from his real life is to tap into devices that sap his energy and dull or scramble his mind. These tempting escapist candies peddled as "fun" include all types of recreational drugs, which include regular and excessive use of marijuana, alcohol, or prescription drugs. They suck out a quantum of energy that would otherwise allow him to jump over the fence and stimulate his brainpower to cope with reality. Thereby, these chemicals contaminate his ability to use good judgment and focus his energy toward productive goals. Cocaine, ecstasy, "molly," and other street drugs are very dangerous and shouldn't even be tried once.

The mind-set of being "stoned" from the chemical effect of ingesting and/or inhaling cannabis is running backward to the unchallenged bliss of the mother's womb. "Stoned"—the ultimate state of "no mind"—describes the distorted bliss of staring blankly at random thoughts that haphazardly pop up within the brain's slowed perception of time.

The effects of drug- and alcohol-induced "relaxation" or the temporary "high" induce a passive state of mind by sucking out the body's natural store of energy; they therefore weaken the connection with reality. "Temporary" is the operative word here. Eventually, the haze wears off, and reality remains. The young man will have to face his daily issues with less energy and money and wasted time.

The 21st century young man will know when to #JustSayNo. He nurtures his mind and energy. Ready to take on tasks and issues, he doesn't hide from them through smoke and haze. He is a warrior who does not say "the bullets aren't there." He knows how to take his challenges head-on, and he can discern when to party wisely.

The Seducer of Seducers: The Digital Media

Another mind-ruling and vigor-emptying activity that is more seductive than chemical cop-outs is the excessive devotion to digital games; pseudosocial, on-screen chatting; and the other numerous digital activities that distract rather than help build mental, physical, and emotional muscle.

Too much media, particularly the visual media, replaces your own thinking and the real-life experiences that belong to you; you end up vicariously living through that athlete or unattainable celebrity. It also keeps you inside the propaganda machine of the media, cramping your creativity. You want to avoid this, especially in the 21st century, which is a time in history when original ideas are rewarded and doors fly open to greater financial and career opportunities.

The Reality Check

The facts about the amount of time the digital media bites out of real living overwhelms common sense. The number of hours boggles the mind and challenges the sanity of the culture. The average American watches television nearly four hours a day.

Recent research found that adults in the United States look at other screens, such as tablets, computers, and smart phones about five additional hours a day. Some may be work-related but may also be for entertainment.

According to a recent pole from CNN and Commen Sense Media "Teens spend a 'mind-boggling' 9 hours a day using media. Let's just put nine hours in context for a second. That's more time than teens typically spend sleeping, and more time than they spend with their parents and teachers. And the nine hours does not include time spent using media at school or for their homework."This begs the question "Who is the real teacher?"

The minimum average given to watching television translates to over 1,233 hours a year, which equates to 140 8-hour days; this is equivalent to 4.5 months of 8-hour days of awake time. This figure only sums up the minimum average and does not include the other five hours a day occupied viewing other forms of digital media.

The Question: Do Hours of Media Viewing Help or Retard?

It takes about ten thousand hours to gain mastery in a skill. The skill can be physical, such as carpentry, welding, general construction, baseball, running, dancing, or downhill skiing.

It can include artistic areas, such as drumming, playing the violin or piano, painting, acting, directing, designing architecture, performing landscape design, and doing many actions. It also includes professional areas, such as practicing medical, teaching, practicing law, computer programming, writing, performing scientific research, and performing military service, just to mention a few. Additionally, business occupations, such as accounting, marketing, sales, management, and investing are other skills that demand many hours of practice to gain competence. The point is that any skill that gets you money and gives you satisfaction requires about ten thousand hours of working at honing the skill to master it.

The 21st century man is conscious of his time and the amount energy expended online, on social media, and on various digital-media time sucks. He is highly knowledgeable and needs to allocate his time by taking care of his studies and/or work so that he may grow and advance his future. While all of his friends and future competitors are being sucked into wasting their time, he is using his ten thousand hours that he isn't on digital platforms to making himself a much stronger and more competent man.

The Choice: Addiction or Addition?

Managing one's time on digital media is a major decision. It is the difference between an addiction *or* an addition. A young man growing into a powerful and fully developed man can certainly discern between the two. Selecting when, how much, and what to do with these precious hours, which cannot be recycled, makes a significant difference in one's success, now and later in life.

It is not that knowledge is power; it is rather that useful knowledge provides the power. This statement means choosing between being passive or active—that is, looking at images on various digital screens for hours or using the hours to master a skill.

Seeking accomplishment and working hard to achieve it is manly. Penetrating, assertive activity is masculine. Passivity does not define manliness. Moreover, to actively choose your goal and seek your purpose is the underlying essence of virility. Not to choose is passive, boyish, and uninteresting, but you do have the freedom to choose whether to be addicted and waste valuable time and energy online or to choose substantial information and activities that add to your welfare (addition). Don't waste your time; it is simply wasting your life.

PLANNING AHEAD: TIMED EVENTS IN A MAN'S LIFE

The Rule of 72

As a young man getting ready to venture out on his own, knowing and learning the rule of 72 would benefit you greatly. There is much to learn online, and it is advisable to get onto credible sites that teach investing and future planning.

However, here are some layman's additions to teach you about the rule of 72. Take the rate of interest (say 6 percent), and then divide it into 72. This equals 12, or the number of years for the investment to double. The formula is simple: rate of interest divided into 72 = number of years to double.

At the 6 percent rate, $10,000 doubles to $20,000 in twelve years. In another twelve years, it grows to $40,000, and so on. At 10 percent interest, the historical-average gain for long-term stock investing, the time is reduced to 7.2 years, and so on.

Saving and investing are not in the curriculum taught in high school or even college. It is up to the 21st century young man to wake up to the benefits of planning ahead. As we stated above, this could be one of those highly valuable online-time investments—to learn about actual investments.

Also seek advice from those whom you trust who have knowledge about investing, and choose wisely for yourself. Don't compound your debt; compound your interest. These figures should wake up a young man to the importance of planning ahead.

Twenties to Thirties: The Start-Up Period

The journey to self-discovery begins to intensify for young men in their twenties through the early thirties. The trials-and-tribulations tests of limits, learning of skills, and forming of habits and attitudes begins. Lessons learned well during this ten-year period (more or less) will give them the fundamental skills and knowledge to help gain mastery and power over the rest of their lives. Lessons that should have been learned but were not assimilated or heeded can break men's lives apart or put them on very bumpy roads. It is a long and rough journey.

A ride on a bumpy road with its delays and mishaps is called suffering. It is not fun. A plan and a map for seeing the journey ahead helps greatly to find ways around the potholes and smooths the ride to the very end. A 21st century young man will read this and ascertain what his best course is.

Assuming that you maintain healthy habits and an intelligent lifestyle, it is very likely that you will be living well into your nineties. Enjoy the journey; just make it a good one.

The Culture's Problem with Young Men

With the onslaught and bombardment of information and images of what masculinity and the "fabricated" man should be, created and trending in the media today, it is no wonder that the images are conflicting, superficial, and made to pick wallets. They contain no substance to improve a young man's growth; in fact, they are quite damaging.

The problem for young men in their twenties to thirties is that today's culture does not instruct them on how to grow into manhood. Society is not providing rituals to clearly mark a transition from being a boy to becoming a man, nor does it teach him what manhood is about. Learning about manhood from some dude online who is muscular and "talks big" isn't learning about manhood. Unfortunately, today's culture ignores the importance of mature men as models and educating young men on how to plan ahead well into their nineties.

Whether their situations involve single mothers trying hard to raise their son(s) or fathers who aren't around enough or are completely absent, young men are turning to media in all forms and are getting tremendous amounts of misinformation. Also, their reluctance to speak to another male about their issues or problems then becomes issues and problems in and of themselves. Falsely salvific images and conflicting messages among young men gleaned from a lack of mature guidance are leading to massive issues and are threats to young men who wish to become full men. Also, the lack of guidelines given by men and great role models, which would otherwise lead young men to maturity, causes them to dart about haphazardly, trying this and that and bumping into one wall or another.

The conventional message to men is this: "Get a job and money. Get a car. Get married, and have kids. Buy a house. Do these, and you will be happy." This is pushed by the culture, which encourages men to pursue these goals. However, the map, the means, the funds, and the support to accomplish these goals are left for so many of our young men to figure out for themselves, instead of them being taught. It ignores a young man's need to plan his financial, personal, and social issues ahead of time; these will surface during the critical stages of his life.

The 21st century young man will discern intelligently what is and is not valuable information, especially online. While it is great to see workouts and read articles on being a man, he is wise enough to know the limits of digesting this information. He will work hard on his immediate objectives: school, work, apprenticeship, and so forth. Most of all, he will search and seek out male role models who have admirable qualities that he wants to internalize and emulate. If they are not in his immediate family or circle of friends, they are out there somewhere, and he will find them. He will know that philosophy and the true nature of religion or spirituality sets up a hierarchy for a more meaningful life, and he will sort out the values worth living for.

Taking Action—The First Step: The Job

The first task for a young man during his twenties is to develop work and social skills in order to become independent and a useful part of the world around him. His full-time job is to find a job that energizes and motivates him, which acts as a message that this work is suited for him. Moreover, uninformed choices can cause a man to pay a very dear price for a long time, especially in this very competitive and complex world.

How does all of this work for you? It requires gaining self-knowledge and using the functions of both sides of the brain. Without understanding what drives you, you will have difficulty matching your dreams with your abilities and opportunities that unfold before you.

Some Habits to Help

<u>Use digital media</u> to work the mind and to learn skills that pay off, not just to thrill the eyeballs. A brain that exercises

problem solving rather than processing sound-bite distractions develops intellectual strength. Muscles exercised regularly grow. This means that you should be consistent in your effort and in learning everything possible about your personality, talent, and limits so that you can discern the dreams that can come true via skill building.

Develop social skills with both genders. Women are more sensitive to social nuances than men, so they can be the better teachers. This is important today, since the prevalence of women in the workplace forces men to interact with them as coworkers, bosses, and subordinates. Men, as a general rule, tend to get along fairly well. However, there may be some issues in the workplace together. When dealing with difficult bosses, teachers, peers, or fellow employees who are unfairly rude to you or don't seem to like you, respect from you goes a long way. Though you may not agree with them, don't get angry or antagonistic, and try to learn how to charm them to be on your side. Better social skills spell less trouble.

Seek the company of adult men. In America today, with nearly five hundred women's professional associations and virtually none for men, finding exclusively male adult company becomes a manly task, indeed. You need to go out of your way to seek out worthwhile adult men to be friends with. Surround yourself with intelligent and interesting men, and become one yourself by networking. Keep the company of as many men who can take you to the next level of your career, within and outside of the workplace. No matter your desired career, there are many ways to network through various organizations with like-minded groups, parties, and work and study groups. Also join all-male groups, such as sport clubs, fraternal orders, and male encounter groups. These are some organizations that are frequently found in cities. In addition to the workplace, find men with higher levels of consciousness. They will help you expand and learn things you don't know.

The Second Step: Your Vision

Uncovering a vision that provides an enduring purpose and guidance throughout life is critical to every man. Without the vision and the masculine energy, his purpose fails. A man is vulnerable to lose his direction to the clever manipulators who suck him in for their own purposes.

Tribal and primitive cultures are more earth-centered than today's glass-and-steel societies. They hold deep wisdom of the masculine soul. A young man in these primitive societies who is uncertain and insecure about his future seeks a vision that guides and motivates his life. Usually, he goes to a remote place, sometimes without food. He stays there by himself in silence until a vision of his true identity captures him. The vision consolidates the conflicts that had scattered his energies. His energies are now focused and unified, giving him strength and self-confidence. The solid vision of the young man's identity is an inner experience.

It is special and individual to him. He has become a man among men because he has learned who he is—he is no longer a boy without inner power or direction. He is respected among men, but this is not due to his accomplishments because he is still too young. The approval is earned because the man who was once a boy has penetrated to the center of his masculine soul and has brought to light his own, unique vision. It then fuels his dreams, forms goals, and strengthens him against wavering off the direction he has set for himself.

Rituals to Manhood

Conversely, the problem for today's modern young male is that there are no clear paths or rituals to help him upload a life vision that will guide him. In primitive societies that have these rituals, the boy is taken from the woman's world and guided through painful and sometimes dangerous ordeals. Once the boy has passed the tests, the men of the tribe declare the boy a man. The rituals teach the boy the following lessons:

1. Life is hard and painful.
2. To survive, you need to achieve.
3. You are part of the tribe, and life is not about you.
4. You are going to die.

These rituals transform the mentality of the boy to another level of understanding. Some of these rituals in tribal cultures imprint these messages on the boy unambiguously. In some aboriginal tribes in Australia, the boy is painted white to remind him of bones and death. He is then placed in a grave and covered with leaves. In other rituals, the boy is placed under blankets "to die," and then his foreskin is cut off.

Young men of the Lakota Sioux tribe set out by themselves on vision quests. They go without food or sleep until visions appear to them, affirming something fundamental to each young man about who he is. This vision is powerful and guides the young man throughout his life. The point of these rituals is that the boy-self is put to death and transformed into a new self—that of a man.

Rituals to Use

You're pretty lucky today in America; no one is going to send you to the forest without food to uncover your life's purpose. In today's buzzing world, a better way to uncover your vision is to separate from the noise that drowns out your inner voice.

Being bored and looking inside yourself is a good thing. Being alone and quiet from media and social chatting allows you to hear your inner truth speak. Stopping the incessant daily interruptions, such as your cell phone, texts, social media obsession, television, and all of the video games, and getting quiet will allow you to get in touch with what you genuinely want and need. This specifically means capturing your vision and your dreams, not those hyped by advertisers, popular media gurus, and music or film idols.

It is your vision, not someone else's. As a 21st century young man, you will get a leg up on everyone else because you will dig to your core to find your truth. You need to be quiet, be alone, and listen to yourself. Find what works for you to get away from all the distractions. Some suggestions that may help in today's noisy society are hiking, visiting the ocean, meditating alone and/or at a spiritual center, practicing yoga (this is great), or going to a retreat of some sort.

Without a Clear Path, How Does a Young Man Become Affirmed as a Man?

The answer is this: not easily.

A few decades ago, it used to be that having marriage and family and owning a home was how society gauged a young man's progress to manhood. The additional challenge for young men transitioning to adult manhood is that a car, an apartment, a decent-paying job, and some spendable money are more difficult to attain. Due to economic conditions, those goals are delayed for many men in their twenties and early thirties in this day and age.

However, there is an action that is necessary to be affirmed as a man. You choose it! And you work to be a complete, 21st century adult man. It means fathering yourself, overcoming obstacles, and hearing your inner truth tell you, "I am a man."

A young man with an ambition to father himself to full manhood is wise to seek help from older, mature, successful men who have triumphed over obstacles because they know the battleground and have survived. They can give important guidance and support. Great men of history provide advice and inspiration also.

An outstanding example of fathering oneself is George Washington. He was eleven when his father died. His lack of money for college did not squash his desire for learning. He studied dancing, fencing, and geometry; he designed military uniforms and wrote the book *The Rules of Civility and Decent Behaviour.* He became an officer at the age of twenty and eventually became commander of the colonial forces. Without his leadership, high-mindedness and perseverance, the thirty-nine men who stood by him and signed the US Constitution would probably have been hanged by the winning British forces. Because he fathered himself, sought learning (including the social graces), and lived by high ethical and moral standards, he did not compromise his ethical code. He was a great model of manhood then and remains so today.

Of course, conditions are radically different now but not the power of broad learning, discipline, self-motivation, ethics, and high-minded goals. As a 21century young man, you should learn to live by these high standards. This will put you in the company of superior men.

PLANNING AHEAD, CONTINUED: TIMED EVENTS TO THE NINETIETH YEAR

Thirties to Forties: Skills Applied
We've covered so much of the twenty- to thirty-year-old growth and responsibilities. Now, let's discuss the next phase in a man's life: job skills, social savvy, an understanding of how the world works, and a balance of work with play that will be paving the road and laying the foundation toward his financial and personal goals.

Career and family, if chosen, occupy a man's effort for this period. The thrust of a man's energy at this time is to acquire, prove, and begin to establish himself in his career. Full success in goals is not yet won; hopefully, though, he is well underway to accomplishing it. These years can act like a dangerous pit that a man climbing up the ladder can fall back into. Too much work, too much coming and going, too much food, too many distractions, not enough sleep or exercise—all the general faults of modern life—deplete physical and mental health and well as lay the groundwork for a crisis around the age of forty-five.

This is what a 21st century man wants to avoid: the "too much"! He will also focus on his self-knowledge and internal growth. He will not allow all of the responsibilities on his shoulders to waylay learning about himself and what truly makes him happy.

Forty to Forty-Five: No Man Is Exempt

Success attained, or lack thereof, has a price. The payment comes from either getting what you want or failing to reach your dreams. At this stage, dragons awake and come out of the inner den of the life not lived. Men become restless, searching, uneasy, and questioning: "Has all this work, family, money grabbing, and acquisition of possessions been worth it?" "Is the rest of my life going to be more of the same?" "If I keep on trudging at the same program, will the dreams I put on the shelf to get where I am ever happen?" "Did I put my ladder against the wrong wall?" These are basic questions that haunt men consciously or unconsciously at these times in their lives.

If a man has channeled all of his energies into achieving, it is more than likely that he has not done his inner homework. Having ignored his feelings and sensitivities, he is likely to fall prey to counterfeit actions that attempt to substitute for the inner void of having missed the mark. Not infrequently, the unbalanced man in his forties travels backward to his adolescence and indulges in its immaturities—sexual exploits with younger women, drugs and drinking, risky sports, high-powered motorcycles, or expensive sports cars.

He can also take an alternative route by signing out of authentic living through a variety of conscious and unconscious behaviors, such as overeating, overworking, drowning his painful thoughts in electronic media, or taking the role of a fanatic for some cause. Marriages may falter because the husband has not grown emotionally. He also may become depressed because an unsatisfying job has sapped his creative energy, preventing him from seeking different avenues to inner contentment.

On the other hand, men who have maintained a habit of looking inside themselves to understand what is really important can move their energy more easily to constructive and productive activities. I know men at this stage who have continued their education, begun doing social work, or taken up painting, fishing, golf, running, or dancing. They did not blame others, seek adolescent thrills, or use artificial ingredients to kill the inner pain of the lives they had to postpone or temporarily surrender. They looked at their souls without denying, ignoring, or excusing what was missing. They acted as mature men. They were able to make constructive choices during these critical five years, which led to feeling great about themselves, all while enhancing their own lives and those for whom they were responsible.

Now, as a 21st century young man who is reading this or perhaps even a man at this stage in his life, you have the insight to manifest your innate potential and not wreak havoc on yourself and those for whom you care.

Fifty-Eight to Seventies: One-Third to Go

This period begins a major revision in a man's perception of himself. During this cycle, a man begins coping with the reality that he has finished the first two-thirds of his life's journey. Regardless of the wishful anecdotes for immortality, the vitamins, workouts, vegetables, and medications, his body begins to talk back.

Assuming that he has done his inner self-exploration and passed the critical tests along the way, and that he has won reasonable success, his material, family, social, and career ambitions are not as demanding on his energies. The urge for a man now is to look at what is really important to him on a nonmaterial level. He has more energy, freedom, and time to question and explore his mortality and his relationship to the divine, however he conceives it. He knows where he has been, where he is going, and how to get there. Dreams put on hold can come alive again.

As a 21st century young man reading this, you may think that this seems a lifetime away. However, the day will come, and you will be prepared, ready, and excited to take this next inner adventure.

Eighty-Four-Plus: Very Likely!

Today, a young man in his twenties or thirties can look forward to an active life well into his nineties. When he reaches his eighties, he should have generated sufficient income and developed absorbing interests, as well as being smart enough to have avoided the traps that mess up a life.

Hopefully, by this time, he has come to terms with the divine as he conceives it. The seasoned man is sailing at full sail on pleasant seas. Of course, physical challenges and loneliness will inevitably arise. Maturity and intelligent living throughout the years will give him the resources to cope with these issues of aging.

THE 21ST CENTURY MAN TAKING ACTION

The Business of the Body

Thus far, we've covered a tremendous amount on how a 21st century man can take care of his status, dealing with fathering himself, relating to the opposite sex, and planning ahead. Yet so much of that won't mean anything without taking care of his body.

It is important to keep the body in good condition and in a high state of physical efficiency because everything a man does is through his body. This commonsense thinking about bodily well-being seems self-evident, but in practice, there is a disconnect. The undeniable evidence for this degrading condition is that obesity plagues men of all ages. A strong and healthy body provides energy and power to a man. Normal weight, sensible diet, and regular exercise are basic priorities necessary to keep fit.

The ancient Romans understood the benefit of this wisdom, *"Mens sana in corpore sano"* or "a sound mind in a sound body." These are great words for the 21st century man to heed if he is awake and values a sound body. He has the mental and emotional muscle to withstand the onslaught of ads designed to seduce him into overeating high-calorie foods that lack nutrition. He has the self-discipline to keep his body lean and fit to look like a fit man.

Not only are the benefits of taking care of yourself important to your health, but in today's society, there is a tremendous amount of respect as well, and it gives you an edge over the competition. Studies done at Harvard University and University of Illinois at Urbana-Champaign's Beckman Institute state clearly that exercise helped tremendously in cognitive abilities, brain heath, and efficacy, which means one's capability to address challenges and accomplish tasks. (Not to mention the hot girls—but we'll get into that later.)

Muscle to the Rescue?

It is widely known that a man's body and greater muscle mass makes him stronger than a female. Do muscles then give him the edge? Not necessarily. Studies have shown that excessively big bulges impress men more than women. When women are asked to choose the body type most appealing to them, they consistently chose the average, fit-guy body type. Of course, every man will choose what he likes and what makes him happy. If you're going for the Arnold Schwarzenegger look, have at it. However, it's not necessary for getting girls or advancing your career. Staying physically fit and even lightly muscular will do the trick and give you a bonus.

Clothes Make and Unmake a Man

Dress to impress. This is a saying that has lasted through the ages. Why? Dressing well is easy, inexpensive, and very effective to help a man advance in almost every activity done around people. Yet most men are indifferent to the way they dress. This is a big mistake. Appearance is an information signal. It stamps a man's quality at first glance. Whether it is accurate, superficial, or misleading, people read a man's frame and how he dresses as a measure of his manliness and competence. The first impression labels him and can stick for a long time.

Your IQ on Parade: Both Sides of Your Brain Working Together

The Wechsler Adult Intelligence Scale, a standard measure of intelligence, adds scores from two separate divisions of mental functions, the verbal and nonverbal abilities, which form the total IQ. The subtests of the nonverbal division are largely loaded to measure visual abilities, which are connected to the right side of the brain. But what does this mean for manly attire? It means a great deal.

People see you before you open your mouth, and they continue to see you at work, in school, and at fun events. Directly or indirectly, everyone who sees you is sizing up your nonverbal IQ on the basis of your looks. The clothes you have on—their fit, style, color, and the degree to which they are relevant to the occasion—transmit, in the blink of an eye, where you belong, where you came from, where you are going, and whether you have the stuff to get there. It is how you are perceived that counts. This can work either to your advantage or disadvantage. Fashion is a visual language (the style, fit, and color); never stop broadcasting as long as you are in view. It is nonverbal communication that speaks volumes.

Throughout history, males have understood the effects of attire and have valued dressing themselves smartly. During two of the most awakening periods in history, the Renaissance and the Enlightenment, men dressed as flamboyantly and elegantly as women. The men of these times, who upgraded civilization, had both sides of their brain working together.

A man of the 21st century hopefully will take clues from great men of the past and will wear clothes that suggest he has both sides of his brain in working order. It would seem that clothes that are the norm today are sloppy, unkempt, and ill-fitting, and they are most often out of sync with the occasion. They are off-putting and reflect a lack of integrated intelligence and blunted social sensitivity.

One study reported that around 63 percent of men and around 72 percent of women rate a disheveled appearance as the number one deal breaker for continuing to date that sloppy individual. It is right up there with laziness. Yet the effect of doing the opposite—being well groomed and neatly dressed, with appropriate style—can welcome women instead of pushing them away. And no man wants to be rejected.

The 21st century young man will take all of this into consideration. He uses both sides of his brain and dresses appropriately for occasions.

The Job You Have and the Job You Want

After my first lecture on business dress as part of a business-communication class that I taught at a California university, I could barely recognize my students. Instead of faded jeans; loose-fitting, randomly colored shirts; unkempt hair; and high-mileage shoes, I saw long-sleeved, clean, white shirts; creased pants; trim haircuts; and polished shoes. I was shocked and very happy to see this turnabout.

These upper-division students were motivated and gobbled up the message because they had already suspected the importance of appearance, which no one had taught them! The details awed them, as if they were once locked-up secrets.

Dress for the job you want, not for the job you have. This is time-tested advice for men who want to advance in their careers. It is a basic business practice. Doing this requires subtle and careful observation, since imitating the boss can backfire if overdone. Stand out cleverly. Less is more in some cases. The 21st century man weighs out, discerns, and evaluates his situation and puts all of this valuable advice to use.

Taking Action: Notching up Your IQ

We know that clothes that fit are flattering. Pants, shirts, and outer garments that are too loose or too tight and are not in proportion to a man's frame declare that a piece of his brain is retarded. High-cost or prestigious labels do not matter a damn if the clothes do not fit properly. Finding the right fit is half the success of dressing well; the rest is the combination and relevance to the occasion.

How do you know that you're hitting the mark? Look in the mirror, and look at others. Take note of good and bad fit, and then make an effort to measure your frame and match your attire to it. Find a tailor to adjust your fit. Small and inexpensive changes can improve your image significantly.

The 21st century man will shop for quality and will research the stores that discount nice clothing. He will dress for success and to impress.

Appropriate for the Event

Jeans, shorts, T-shirts, and cargo pants at church services, the opera, tango events, or anniversary or birthday celebrations are not out of the ordinary in today's dressed-down culture. This is appalling! Out-of-sync dress like this is insensitive, reflecting a dull wit and lack of social IQ. It shows that you do not get it, just like someone who wears a suit and tie to the beach, faux fur in eighty-degree weather, or a T-shirt at the prom.

At the very least, out-of-sync dress, no matter how commonly it occurs, will not open doors or lubricate ones that are stuck, unless you have a lot of power, money, or a goody that someone is greedy for. Proper dress shows respect, not only for the person who invited you, but for yourself, too.

Shoes

Women, job recruiters, and employers never miss looking at shoes. They add up the shoes' polish, quality, fit, and style to size up the candidate. If all other parts of dress score a passing grade, lousy shoes get an F. The impression given by scruffy or low-grade shoes says that something about you is not together and that you are not aware of important details. Although this may not necessarily be the truth about you, it is often mistaken as a fact that implies that your competence is suspect.

Pay attention to the quality of your shoes, and keep them polished and clean. There are many shoe-repair stores that are inexpensive and will keep your shoes looking good.

Style

Style comes from consciousness and character. It serves as a medal of honor from learning about yourself and achieving a goal important to you. Style marks you as an individual who has not followed the crowd and who has had the courage to respect desires special to yourself. Copying everyone else's fashion is foolish because it broadcasts that you are dancing to everyone else's tunes and not your own. The effort a man puts forth to learn his own truth, develop his abilities, and expand his awareness gives rise to his own style. Not only is this true in dress but also in his manner of living.

The 21st century man's style reflects his uniqueness, his distinction, and his evolving awareness.

Grooming: Absolute Turnoffs

* Nose hairs are considered worse than bad breath, which a man definitely does not want.
* Messy hair and unkempt facial hair announces that you are still growing out of puberty. Messy beards are

okay for mountain men, but in the city, men do not have to wrestle bears. Beards should be neatly trimmed and squeaky clean.

* Dirty fingernails as well as dirt in general are unacceptable.
* Bad breath and overuse of smelly cologne are unacceptable.

Keep in mind that although women are repelled by poor grooming, they are reluctant to criticize it directly, for fear of offending the male ego. So more than likely, they simply won't answer your calls.

You're a strong, 21st century young man, and you're probably aware of these turnoffs. So let's get you turned on and into the habit of consistent, good grooming. These are the very basics, so do your due diligence and research online as well as utilize men's magazines, as they generally give good tips about grooming.

LEARNING HOW TO MULTIPLY MONEY

Young men in their twenties are rarely concerned about investing. Most have hardly enough play money as it is. Then the costs of tuition, books, and living expenses leave little cash to squeeze out of the budget. Of course, the hope is to get financial momentum while learning a job skill and working toward the future. But that could take ten or twenty years before the money gets into the bank.

Job stability with retirement is history. Today's norm for many young men is hopping from job to job, hopping from project to project, and performing independent contracting. The government, given its debt, is near its tipping point already. The private sector is not reliable. Men working in this century's economic model need to secure their own financial independence. Due to the fast-paced job turnover, young men should consider developing multiple sources of income (stocks, bonds, part-time jobs, online sales) while working toward their career paths. Investing early in life puts a young man far ahead of the game in developing alternative sources of income.

It is far better to learn how to multiply money now than ten or twenty years down the road. Recall the rule of 72 and the magic of compound interest. Using 1 to 5 percent of the cash you have in hand and working to make it grow in the stock market, real estate, or in collectibles can pay off substantially in the long run. There is little to lose during the early stages of learning an investment technique, mostly because you will start with smaller dollar amounts until you get your footing.

Keep in mind, however, that chances are that you will lose some dollars while exercising your investing plans. This is inexpensive tuition, for learning how money works for you at this stage not only helps bring large gains later on but also (most importantly) teaches lessons to help save you from losing large sums you have accumulated through the years. Do not fear making mistakes. Failure is just another learning tool. You will lose little money in the beginning because you will not have much to lose. In any case, investments rarely fall to zero, and some money should remain for another day.

COLLEGE AND TUITION

Unless your parents pay for it, college is a very expensive place to make mistakes while struggling to find your occupation, position in the world, and the kind of people you belong with. College can cost tens of thousands of dollars or even more. Then, you may graduate, only to discover that you are not equipped to make your first dream a practical reality. Another fact to keep in mind is that most men rarely end up doing what they set out to do.

Some Possibilities
Though only one-third of jobs require college degrees, it is an important ticket for a job interview. A young man intent on success cannot ignore this issue. Unless you are 110 percent sure about your major and what you wish to do for a living, there are some ways to maneuver around the problem of indecision.

Courses at community colleges provide opportunities for testing interests and abilities at reasonable costs. Entry-level jobs in some businesses or occupations can give inside looks at the abilities and demands required. Volunteer work and/or apprenticeships can give training as well as overviews of work opportunities. Traveling abroad for six months can give more education than four years in a university, with the bonus of discovering how the real world works. Also, tuition in colleges and universities in other parts of the world, especially in Europe, are less expensive than in the United States. Doing research online about top-ranking colleges abroad will garner much surprising information about the education standards and reduced costs.

The 21st century young man looks forward and is alert to the new paths forming in this century. For a young man to do this well, he should seek all the help he can get. Asking questions is a technique many successful men use, but unfortunately, many young men do not. Ask, research, and think. Why? Because most young men have an aversion to seek advice from older, successful, and more mature men. But those beginning their journeys can gain years and even decades of advanced knowledge that can accelerate the achievements of their goals.

For those who aren't going to college and seeking an apprenticeship or work with a specific company, do your research and learn everything you can. Find a secure and successful man whom you admire, who works in the field that interests you, if not for the company you wish to work with directly.

Dress neatly and appropriately in order to give the impression that you are serious and that you respect his authority. Recall that your appearance flags you, for better or worse, and that the impression sticks.

Here is a suggested opening statement: "I am a student, a recent graduate, and I am interested in learning about your work and your company. Can you please help me understand about the business culture here and the goals of the company?"

Persistence in doing this can win an apprenticeship, a job, or at the very least, some valuable information. There is absolutely nothing to lose, and it is a sure win on some level.

THE HUMANITIES FOR INTELLIGENT LIVING

The humanities teach how and why humans behave and misbehave. They include but are not limited to literature, philosophy, the visual arts, the performing arts, music, anthropology, history, religious studies, languages, and political science.

The humanities pierce to the core of the human condition. They teach how people think, feel, act, and react. They look at people's motivations, faults, values, and common needs. They give insight into what is really valuable in life. In this new era of our global world, they are also particularly practical. Understanding the human situation in different cultures and having good social skills have become important raw materials for operating in today's multicultural economy.

Another reason to consider the benefits of studying the humanities are jobs that are interpersonal and one-on-one and those that require—even demand—interaction with people. Because the humanities specialize in communication skills and knowledge about people, they may help you to avoid stepping on social land mines. It could mean the difference between being welcomed and appreciated instead of being disliked and rejected.

Sixty percent of US CEOs have degrees in the humanities. A study made of three million Americans, schooled in the humanities, found that those between the ages of fifty-five to sixty-five (the highest earning years) made more than those who had majored in professional studies.

The 21st century young man certainly needs as much leverage in today's competitive society, and learning the humanities will certainly impart that.

Human behavior flows from three main sources: Desire, emotion and knowledge.
—Plato

We've spoken in depth about learning the arts and humanities and the benefits men glean from gaining knowledge about human behavior, much less about themselves. Plato said it best when he stated that it flows from three main sources: desire, emotion, and knowledge.

Some men do thrive financially in business and technical jobs without any special interest in human studies. Their focus is primarily on work and just about nothing else, and that concentrated energy gains their goals. However, often, the only thing worse than not getting what you want is getting what you want. This is especially true when the effort to get what you desire is only channeled in one direction. One-sided focus has a price and comes with dangers. When a man does not understand himself and the deeper sensitivities of others, he sets himself up for defeating traps of his own making.

He may discover that, after many long years of not looking up or around, it's very lonely. Perhaps he is rich in the bank but not in the soul. His need for material success sacrificed and soured his interior wealth and his enjoyment of many valuable experiences. Men who have not attended to their emotional awareness frequently encounter dangers at the forty-five-year mark. Clashes in the work place, ill health, divorce, the effects of chasing much younger women, and even early death upon retirement are perhaps the most common dangers.

The 21st century man does not have a one-sided focus toward an unbalanced life. His greatest aim is the art of knowing how to live well and wisely, especially for the long term. He will balance his emotions, desires, and knowledge while navigating his way through his career and reaching the top.

LIFELONG LEARNING

Adjusting throughout life, and especially during this dynamic 21st century, is a nonstop dance. In order to stay balanced and adjusted, a man needs to study, listen, practice, perform, draw, paint, and play consistently in any branch of human studies that captures his interest. Literature, history, philosophy, art, and theater are just a few.

Lifelong learning is lifelong thinking. It's not just about what you learned in school or what the media is teaching and preaching. Though valuable to a point and stage in one's life, it is also about challenging the values and worth of the changes enveloping you that incessantly and irrevocably occur on this planet. Be awake.

Another benefit of keeping abreast is having the advantage to sniff out what is new before everyone else knows about it and using what you learn to your advantage. This gives you foresight and an edge. A 21st century young man stays awake and constantly alert. He is learning, growing, and looking ahead for the changes that can affect him, both personally and collectively.

CONCLUSION

As I wrote this book, I didn't have a doubt that the young men of the 21st century can lead; I just knew that they needed more direction. The developments happening during the beginning of the 21st century are turning many values, beliefs, attitudes, policies, and institutions upside down. Technological, economic, social, political, and environmental shifts are forcing a rethinking and reorientation. Young men of today are the leaders in this world. They are in positions to make changes happen and to reset the courses of ineffective and destructive conditions that are happening.

They are the future. The problem standing in the way of young men, who are readjusting the course of events in our future, is that they, too, are changing with the changing times because neither their roles nor positions are clear or stable. They are coming to terms with past ideas and ideals of manhood. The rising power of women; the shortage of supportive, adult men to give constructive direction; and the economic limitations have diminished young men's abilities to become self-sufficient and honored.

Rethinking the ideal of manhood now offers opportunity for a young man honestly to say again to himself, "I am a man." Strong, complete, and full manhood is within reach of courageous young men who are raising their consciousness. Achieving the goal of being a man who is successful in the material world, while not losing touch with the space inside of himself, requires a long-term commitment.

Striving to be a full, balanced, and mature man is challenging and demanding. It demands the courage to think for yourself rather than following the crowd and to accept the wisdom to learn from your mistakes and the mistakes of others, as well as from losing and succeeding. It is a wise decision that you will make: to take on the purpose of becoming a full and strong man, both emotionally and physically.

The choice you are making is brave because the tribe and society no longer provide clear guidelines, male role models, or rituals to grow from boyhood to manhood, especially to a well-rounded and balanced one.

THE 21ST CENTURY WARRIOR

It is a formidable struggle for the young man in this 21st century world to win success and attain the deep satisfaction and contentment that a complete, mature, and accomplished man enjoys. Overcoming the complexities, rapid changes, and ever-increasing barriers that confront young men today commands courage, physical stamina, discipline, knowledge, and foresight. Conquering the immediate, visible, and cleverly disguised obstacles opposing him demands these virtues and, most especially, the deeply seated masculine power of the warrior. He will need to face up to and win against the forces surrounding his freedom and well-being, in order to be the complete, full, mature man for whom this century begs.

Today's evolved warrior is different from those of the past. He sets out to be a man on his own terms. He does not take orders blindly from others who use him for their own agendas. He questions the dictates of authorities—political, educational, religious, and medical, and especially media propaganda and popular hype—to sort out whether their programs fit into the benefit of his independence and security of his future.

This is serious business for any man who will let all the neurons fire on both sides of his brain. History, past and present, has been and continues to be rife with incompetent judgments, ideas, and decisions that lead to obstruction, difficulty, destruction, and death. The "change" these "captains of the people" tout to "make things better" is always suspicious. These powerful elites rarely look at the facts squarely and almost never tell the truth to those who support them.

Moreover, they most often lack the self-insight that would allow them to overcome their self-interest for the common good. This is indeed a jaundiced view of many who lead. Read history, and take a good look at the behavior of the nineteenth and twentieth centuries if you may think this statement is exaggerated. Who knew this better than Hitler? "The masses are effeminate and stupid," he said. He wanted power, and he manipulated the minds of men.

However, look at Franklin D. Roosevelt. Though crippled with polio, he stood strong with determination and foresight to create very powerful governmental policies that altered the course of Americans' lives, despite the immense challenges he faced both physically and professionally during his entire political career.

So the 21st century warrior uses all of his faculties (mind, body, spirit) and is cognizant of what is happening around him. Knowing himself, he has a plan to accomplish his vision, which he has uncovered from within. His expanded consciousness and high standards set him apart from the common herd and various purveyors of misaligned ideas and orders.

The 21st century man uses his intelligence to climb higher. He joins the company of aspiring and great-minded men from all ages, drawing from the reservoir of their deep, unbounded masculine energy. Thus, he is empowered and fights for the dignity, respect, and lives of others and himself. By just his intention and effort to become a whole and mature man, as his abilities and circumstances allow, he helps guide this new century to a better place than the destructive and badly behaved two centuries of the past. A new order? A new paradigm? *Yes.*

A 21st century man is very much like a fine sword that is tempered and made with the highest standard of quality metals that can withstand strong and opposing blows. He is able to take the best qualities he sees in other men and in himself and forge them into a man of steel.

RECOMMENDED READING

Highly Recommended:
Dieda, David. *The Way of the Superior Man: A Spiritual Guide to Mastering the Challenge of Women, Work, and Sexual Desires.* Sounds True, 2004.

Blogs:
MGTOW: Men Going Their Own Way
About men empowering themselves and owning their own lives. Take the red pill. It will spin your head around regarding the female.

The Art of Manliness
http://www.artofmanliness.com/
A website worth reading weekly.

For the Job:
Allen, Jeffery G. *How to Turn an Interview into a Job.* Simon and Schuster, 1985.

REFERENCES FOR MANNERS AND STYLE

Etiquette for Dummies
Sue Fox
Wiley Publishing, Inc.

Modem Manners: Tools to Take You to the Top
Dorothea Johnson and Liv Taylor
Crown Publishing Group, 2013

Indulgent: The Complete Style Guide for the Modern Man
Jeff Lack
New Holland Publishers, 2013

REFERENCES CONCERNING MEN

Is There Anything Good about Men?
Roy F. Baumeister
Oxford University Press, 2010

The Secret Life of Men: A Practical Guide to Helping Men Discover Health, Happiness, and Deeper Personal Relationships
Steve Biddulph
Da Capo Press, 2003

Absent Fathers, Lost Sons: The Search for Masculine Identity
Guy Corneau
Shambhala Publications, Inc., 1991

Fatherless America: Confronting Our Most Urgent Social Problem
David Blankenhorn
Harper Perennial, 1996

Average Is Over: Powering America Beyond the Age of the Great Stagnation
Tyler Cowen
The Penguin Group
Dutton 2013

Why Men Are the Way They Are
Warren Farrell
Berkley Books/Published by McGraw Hill
New York, 1986

The Myth Of Male Power
Warren Farrell
Berkley Books/Simon and Schuster
New York, 1993

Women Can't Hear What Men Don't Say
Warren Farrell
Tarcher/Penguin 1999

The Seasons Of A Man's Life
David J. Levinson
Ballantine Books/Random House Publishing Group, 1978

Adam's Return
Richard Rohr
Crossroad Publishing Co., 2004

Men on Strike: Why Men Are Boycotting Marriage, Fatherhood, and the American Dream—and Why It Matters
Helen Smith, PhD
Encounter Books, New York, 2013
Statistics and Additional Data

Suicide Statistics
https://afsp.org/about-suicide/suicide-statistics/

College Statistic
https://www.washingtonpost.com/news/storyline/wp/2014/12/11/women-are-dominating-men-at-college-blame-sexism/?utm_term=.3be70e9f703e
https://www.bostonglobe.com/metro/2016/03/28/look-how-women-outnumber-men-college-campuses-nationwide/YROqwfCPSlKPtSMAzpWloK/story.html
https://www.google.com/url?sa=t&rct=j&q=&esrc=s&source=web&cd=4&cad=rja&uact=8&ved=0ahUKEwiwh-fd6uPUAhXKPiYKHRCJD-wQFggxMAM&url=https%3A%2F%2Fwww.forbes.com%2Fsites%2Fccap%2F2012%2F02%2F16%2Fthe-male-female-ratio-in-college%2F&usg=AFQjCNEpdMOMamSxx1ijeA4wZvBTzl8ZzQ

Doctors And Lawyers Stats
https://www.theatlantic.com/sexes/archive/2012/12/more-women-are-doctors-and-lawyers-than-ever-but-progress-is-stalling/266115/

Median Full Time Salaries Statistics
http://content.time.com/time/business/article/0,8599,2015274,00.html

Men Portrayed Negatively In The Media
https://www.forbes.com/sites/meghancasserly/2012/11/14/are-men-the-latest-victims-of-media-misrepresentation/#b3e30322caf0

Teens & Media
http://www.cnn.com/2015/11/03/health/teens-tweens-media-screen-use-report/index.html
https://www.commonsensemedia.org/sites/default/files/uploads/pdfs/census_factsheet_televisionandvideoviewing habits.pdf
Robots and Jobs
http://www.businessinsider.com/experts-predict-that-one-third-of-jobs-will-be-replaced-by-robots-2015-5

ACKNOWLEDGMENTS

I salute and thank the hundreds of young men and women who laid bare their concerns to me. Without their courage and honesty to express issues important to them, I would be angling for trout rather than trying to light a candle within the current cultural chaos. I would especially like to thank writer and publicist Nadine Christine Hamdan, whose insight and fun personality certainly made the process enjoyable, enlightening, and profitable.

For their support and advice, special thanks to Peter Deyell of the Director's Guild, Sonobol Moini, and Quin Redeker for their help. Keith Klein's insights were as beneficial to me as his expertise in illustrating and designing this book.

Visit me on the web: www.themanyoucanbeforthe21stcentury.com.
© 2017 The Man You Can Be For The 21st Century. All Rights Reserved.

ABOUT THE AUTHOR

J. D. Lee, better known as Douglas Lee to his friends and work associates, served as a school and educational psychologist for three decades. Working for both the private and public sectors, J. D. made his way in and out of the minds of young men and women, empowering, expanding, guiding, and counseling them toward constructive behavior and getting them on the right paths. From the late teens to early twenties, both formally and socially, J. D. helped young men and women develop, grow and become productive.

In his youth, J. D. grew up in a residential, agricultural area in Los Angeles, with horses, sheep, and animals on the family property. Instead of television, he would spend much of his time outdoors, riding his horses and tending to all of the animals before and after school. He fondly remembers this wonderful time, when he developed into a responsible young man with integrity.

Attending an all-boys high school at Notre Dame, he had a classical education and went through a disciplined environment, taking his studies seriously. His teachers were former GIs and religious brothers who would teach in a very strict but fair manner. Having seen the worst of humanity, they knew the value of life and didn't put up with nonsense or superficiality. This imparted a great deal of strength for J. D. to grow up with, as well as discipline, clarity of vision, purpose, and a desire for learning. He wouldn't waffle when presented with challenges as an adult, because he was taught by strong men how to grow in mental and moral strength.

At the age of nineteen, J. D. would take his education further and would enroll in Notre Dame University, already knowing that he would major in psychology. He worked hard on his education, graduating from UCLA and finishing off with a master's degree from Cal State. After graduation, he taught special education and earned his credentials as a school and educational psychologist.

J. D. would spend most of his career in senior high schools all over the great expanse of the Los Angeles school district.

From the overprivileged to the underprivileged schools, he covered the socioeconomic spectrum as a school psychologist, dealing with numerous ethnic groups that, in some cases, were complex. From the mixed energies at Hollywood High to very conservative residential areas, J. D. dealt with diverse, disturbed, and (in some cases) gifted young minds.

Dealing with a variety of disorders, J. D. had to discern what was best for a lot of different personalities and make decisions that were very challenging and, in many cases, had legal impacts. However, one of the greatest rewards in his career was when a student came up to him and said, "Thank you for saving my life." His mission to help guide the students and get them on their paths successfully was truly a passion for him.

J. D. developed a peer-counseling program within the continuation high schools. He taught students basic social-interaction skills on how to relate to each other and overcome shyness.

While he has a true passion as a psychologist and fought in the trenches with his students, he left his work at work. His personal life is colorful, exciting, and rich in friendships. His mother's second marriage to one of the most famous musicians had J. D. rubbing elbows with Hollywood celebrities. While not easily impressed by money or celebrity status, he loves being social. One of his greatest passions is having very elaborate parties, which a large variety of eclectic people, artists, dancers, writers, and entrepreneurs attend. A sophisticated man of good taste who can navigate well inside or outside the establishment, J. D. really resonates with people on so many levels. His favorite motto is "joy de vivre."

An ever-evolving man, J. D. resurrected his piano lessons later in life, becoming proficient in ragtime piano. His passion for fly-fishing would take him to eight countries, and his desire to expand his mind and learn about various cultures saw him travel to over fifty countries. He also studied art in Italy and a received a scholarship through the Maryland Institute of Art in 1993, and he studied for month, painting watercolors in Sorrento, Pompeii, and Herculaneum in Southern Italy. Now, his home graces murmurs of beautiful painting he has done with his own two hands and imagination.

J. D. is an avid collector of fly-fishing paraphernalia, rare fishing books, and Civil War swords. His passion for reading and studying Jungian psychology and mythology started in his teens and stayed with him throughout his life. Impassioned and dedicated, he was one of the first to attend the inauguration of the Joseph Campbell Library at Pacifica Institute in Santa Barbara. To this day, he is a student of alchemy and art. With thousands of books in this library, from psychology to astrology, J. D. has a consistent hunger for knowledge and growth; it is still a very intriguing aspect of his life. He is ever evolving and growing in awareness of higher consciousness.

INDEX

* 21st century, 2, 4, 7, 9, 21-22, 32, 42, 46-49, 53, 56, 61, 63, 65-71, 73-79, 81-88, 91-92, 95-97, 100-102, 105, 107, 112-113, 116-118, 120-121, 123-127, 131, 134, 136-137, 139, 141-143, 153
* 4th Dimensional Man, 92, 96, 98
* Absent, 14-16, 21, 94, 106
* Accomplish(ed), 22-23, 30, 49, 103, 107, 110, 115, 121, 141-142
* Achieve, 4, 20-23, 48, 54, 86, 97, 103, 111, 131
* Action, 7-9, 23, 27-28, 30-31, 35, 50, 52, 54, 67, 69, 87 88, 90, 95, 102, 108, 113, 116, 120, 124, 133
* Advice, 3, 7, 25, 30, 32, 47, 75, 105, 114, 124, 131, 153
* Answers, 3, 87
* Balance, 36, 48, 54, 67, 94, 115, 136-137, 140
* Bashing, 64-66
* Benefits, 9-10, 16, 24, 105, 121, 133, 135
* Body, 7, 33, 40, 53, 77, 100, 118, 120-121, 142
* Challenge(s), 10, 17, 22, 37, 49, 51-52, 54, 56, 61, 67, 70, 80, 95, 99-101, 113, 118, 121, 142
* Communication, 30, 32-33, 68, 70, 123-124, 133

159

* Complete, 11, 36, 49, 67, 84-85, 98, 106, 113, 140-141
* Confidence, 21, 30, 34-35, 42, 49, 110
* Connect, 3-4, 14, 22, 30, 39, 48, 74, 87, 100, 122
* Dating, 36, 39, 45, 49-50
* Delinquent elephants, 14-15
* Energy, 6-7, 9, 14, 20, 24, 27, 40, 44, 46, 52, 54, 58, 59, 88, 91, 97, 99-100, 102, 103, 110, 115, 117-118, 120, 125, 135, 143
* Experience, 2-3, 9, 13, 21, 24, 27, 30-31, 39
* Father, 13-16, 18-23, 25, 43, 57, 59, 65, 94, 106, 113-114, 120
* Fathering yourself, 19-21, 23, 113
* Female, 2, 6, 16, 26-28, 30, 34-35, 37-39, 41-32, 44-46, 48, 50, 52-53, 59, 121
* Growth, 2-3, 9, 16, 25, 29, 55, 56, 67, 69, 75-76, 82, 90, 98, 102-104, 106, 109, 115-117, 126, 129, 137, 140, 156, 158
* Health, 10, 23, 43, 57, 60-61, 63, 66-67, 74-75, 106, 115, 120-121, 135
* Identity, 3, 20, 24, 26-29, 93, 110
* Impacting, 56, 59

* Leaders, 4, 11, 76, 114, 139
* Learn, 8-10, 22-23, 30-32, 34, 36, 38-39, 41, 46, 49, 51, 53, 55, 61, 71, 83-85, 87, 98, 104-106, 108-110, 114, 116, 126, 128-129, 131-132, 134-135, 137, 140, 156, 158
* Love, 7, 34, 42, 50, 53-54, 94, 157
* Male, 1-2, 6-7, 10, 13-17, 19-20, 22, 24-28, 30-32, 34-35, 37-39, 41, 44, 46, 50, 52, 54, 56-57, 59, 61, 63-67, 76, 87, 91-94, 96-98, 106-107, 109-111, 123, 127, 140
* Manhood, 2, 13, 14
* Manners, 17, 36, 48, 50, 52, 53
* Masculine, 1, 14, 16-18, 27, 46, 48-49, 55, 58, 66, 91, 103, 110-111, 141, 143
* Media, 5, 11, 22, 30-31, 33, 35, 57, 62-67, 100-103, 106-108, 112, 117, 137, 141
* Mentor, 24-25
* Money, 16, 22, 42, 47, 50, 66, 74, 76, 78, 90, 91-96, 100, 102, 107, 113, 114, 116, 125, 128-129, 157
* Mother, 2, 6-7, 16, 19, 43, 47, 99, 106, 157

The Man You Can Be For The 21st Century

- Opportunity, 45, 50, 80, 91, 140
- Rejection, 35, 38, 65
- Sex, 3, 13, 16, 26-34, 38, 41, 44-46, 49, 54, 58, 64, 93, 97, 116, 120
- Sexuality, 13, 26-27, 46, 58
- Shyness, 31, 33-35, 39, 52, 157
- Skills, 7, 9-10, 17, 22, 24, 30-32, 51, 65, 83, 85-87, 96-97, 102, 105, 108-109, 115, 133-134 157
- Society, 2, 10-11, 28, 45, 51, 56-57, 70, 76, 79, 86, 92-93, 95, 105, 112-113, 121, 134, 140
- Spiritual, 36, 67, 69, 90, 93, 97, 107, 112, 142,
- Strong, 7, 9-10, 21, 56, 70, 87, 89, 96, 98, 102, 120-121, 127, 140, 142-143, 156
- Style, 60-61, 63, 65, 69, 106, 122, 123, 125-126
- Suicide, 57-59

- Unique, 11, 13, 19-20, 97, 111, 126
- Warrior, 59, 67, 89, 92, 100, 141-142
- Whole, 39, 49, 51, 67, 74, 76, 87, 90, 98, 143
- Women, 1-4, 6, 13, 30, 31-33, 35-36, 38-43, 45-52, 54, 56-58, 60-64, 91, 109, 116, 121, 123, 125, 127, 135, 139
- Work, 3, 7-11, 13, 20-25, 33-36, 41-44, 46-47, 49-51, 53, 58, 62-64, 66-68, 71-72, 74, 75, 79-80, 83-87, 92, 94-97, 101-103, 107-110, 112-113, 115-118, 122-123, 128-129, 131-132, 135, 145
- Young Men 1-7, 13-16, 20, 23, 25-27, 30-32, 34, 38, 41, 47, 51, 59, 68, 70, 74, 85, 95, 105-107, 111, 113, 128, 131, 139-141, 153, 155, 156

Made in the USA
Columbia, SC
29 October 2018